The Hardest Walk

By
Bryan Smith

MAPLE
PUBLISHERS

The Hardest Walk

Author: Bryan Smith

Copyright © 2025 Bryan Smith

The right of Bryan Smith to be identified as author of this work has been asserted by the author in accordance with section 77 and 78 of the Copyright, Designs and Patents Act 1988.

First Published in 2025

ISBN 978-1-83538-727-6 (Paperback)
978-1-83538-728-3 (Hardback)
978-1-83538-729-0 (E-Book)

Book Book Cover and Layout by:
White Magic Studios
www.whitemagicstudios.co.uk

Published by:
Maple Publishers
Fairbourne Drive, Atterbury,
Milton Keynes,
MK10 9RG, UK
www.maplepublishers.com

The views expressed in this work are solely those of the author and do not reflect the opinions of Publishers, and the Publisher hereby disclaims any responsibility for them. This book should not be used as a substitute for the advice of a competent authority, admitted or authorized to advise on the subjects covered.

A CIP catalogue record for this title is available from the British Library.

CONTENTS

Introduction 4

Acknowledgment 6

Chapter 1 – The Fear That Shaped Me 7

Chapter 2 – Fighting to Survive 16

Chapter 3 – Taking on Giants 20

Chapter 4 – Betrayal 30

Chapter 5 – Moving On 34

Chapter 6 – My Journey Continues… 39

Chapter 7 – A Fresh Start 45

Chapter 8 – Opportunity 49

Chapter 9 – Family of Three! 52

Chapter 10 – The Ultimate Betrayal 60

Chapter 11 – A Health Anxiety Journey 65

Chapter 12 – Getting Stronger 75

Chapter 13 – Making things better 84

Chapter 14 – My Story Isn't Over 92

Chapter 15 – It's Just the Beginning 104

Introduction

Mental health has long been a conversation we've been too afraid to have. It's messy, unpredictable, and often misunderstood. I'm not writing this as an expert or as someone who has figured it all out. I'm not here with a neat set of steps for you to follow or a perfectly packaged solution. I'm just a person—a person who's spent the better part of my life wrestling with mental health, who still finds themselves struggling with it every day, but who has also learned to survive it. I'm here to talk about my journey, which—like so many others—hasn't been a straight path but a winding, sometimes jagged road filled with potholes, detours, and moments of clarity.

There is no sugar-coating in this book, and no pretence that every day will be better than the last. This is not recovery from a broken leg! Some days, victory is just getting your head off the pillow. Other days, it can feel like a losing or even a lost battle. That's the unvarnished truth. There is no such thing as a quick fix, and the idea that you can "get over yourself" or just "get a grip" is not just unrealistic, it's hurtful and harmful. Mental illness doesn't respect timelines or care if you are a real go-getter or super successful individual or how well you've been able to disguise your struggle. It is persistent and unforgiving, and, for many of us, it is a constant companion.

This book is for those of us who have been living with the unseen. For those who have fought through panic attacks in the middle of a crowded room, or spent nights staring at the ceiling, convinced that the weight of the world is resting squarely on their shoulders. It's for the people who have learned to smile on the outside while their minds are a battlefield. It's for the people who have learned that "getting better" isn't about perfection—it's about persistence. It's about showing up each day, even when your body and mind are telling you to quit.

In these pages, you will read the unfiltered story of my mental health journey. I'll share the moments of despair, but also the quiet victories. I'll talk about the times when I felt completely and utterly lost, and the moments when something inside me clicked, and I remembered that there was hope, even if it felt far away. This isn't a guide to a quick fix. There are no promises here of an easy path. But what I can offer you is the truth: You are not alone. We are not alone.

We are all fighting something, even when we don't talk about it. And that is the point of this book: To show that there is strength in vulnerability. There is strength in admitting that we are not okay. There is power in sharing our struggles with others, in showing up for each other in our brokenness. I don't have all the answers, but together, I hope we can begin to find some peace in knowing that it's okay to be not okay.

So, if you're reading this, know that I see you. I hear you. I am you. And we're in this together.

Acknowledgment

I would like to take this opportunity to express my deepest and most heartfelt gratitude to Deb, my Mum, and my Auntie, who I affectionately refer to as "Sis," for their unwavering, constant support throughout my life. Their love and encouragement have been an absolute cornerstone in helping me navigate the challenges I have faced. I also want to honour my hero in Heaven, my Grandad, whose memory, and strength continue to inspire me every single day. His guidance, even from afar, has shaped who I am today.

In addition, I feel immense gratitude towards Susie Gigg, who I can only describe as "just Heavenly." Her support and guidance during some of my darkest times were truly invaluable. Her presence and care have helped me find a way through difficult moments, and I will always be thankful for the pivotal role she played in my life.

I would also like to extend my sincere appreciation to Bristol Community Services and Rethink Mental Illness for their ongoing support. The work they do has been a source of comfort and stability, and their dedication to improving lives does not go unnoticed.

On a more personal note, I have now had the privilege of working for a company for over ten years, where I feel genuinely valued and respected. I am given the freedom to do my job without unnecessary interference, which has been incredibly empowering. To all my colleagues and managers who supported me when I had hit rock bottom, I am profoundly grateful. Their understanding and encouragement at my lowest points helped me rise again and continue to move forward. Their belief in me has been invaluable, and I will forever appreciate their kindness and support.

Chapter One

The Fear That Shaped Me

Let me set the stage for you. I'm not a writer, a mental health professional, or an expert. I'm just someone who's lived through 40 years of battling mental health challenges. I'm still learning, still struggling, still understanding. But I'm also healing. Slowly, imperfectly, and relentlessly....

It's been a long road, one that I never thought would stretch so far. But here I am, still walking, still fighting, still trying to find my way. And I'm not perfect, nor am I cured. Some days, it feels like I'm back at square one, but the difference now is that I know I'm not alone in this. I know that these battles don't have to be fought in silence anymore. There's power in sharing our stories, and that's what I want to do here—share mine, in all its glorious messiness.

I've got issues—lots of them. Maybe you do, too. And here's the truth I've discovered: We are not alone in this. Mental health doesn't discriminate. It doesn't care who you are, where you've been, or how much you've achieved. And it doesn't just "go away" because someone tells you to "snap out of it." If it were that simple, we'd all be healed by now.

This book is not sugar-coated. It's raw and real because that's what mental health is. No one tells you about the sleepless nights, the days spent battling your own mind, or the constant, unshakable feeling that something's wrong, even when everything around you seems fine. On paper, I might seem like your average guy—happy, functioning, normal. But for decades, I've been haunted by social anxiety, PTSD, depression, and more.

People tell me doubtfully that I don't "look" like someone who struggles. If only they knew how much worse that makes it—feeling invisible while being consumed from the inside.

Mental health issues can take over your life without warning. One minute, you're going about your day, and the next, it's like the ground is pulled from beneath you, and you can't breathe. It's overwhelming. People say they understand, but most don't. And that's okay. We don't need everyone to get it. What we do need is to remind ourselves and each other that we are stronger than we realise. Some days, we can fight back. Other days, we can't. But every single day is a chance for progress. Some days, just getting out of bed is a victory, and that's okay too.

I've nearly spent my entire life searching for answers. From my very first counselling session at 15 to now, nearing 50, I am continuing the search. I've tried therapy, medications, and long walks to keep myself afloat. Those walks inspired me to create "The Walking Man from Bristol" in 2019 - a Facebook page - a space to share journeys, raise awareness and fundraise for others struggling, some even more than me.

The idea for "The Walking Man" came to me during one of those long, lonely walks when I thought about the people I'd met along the way, the people who had shared their struggles with me. I thought; What if we could create a space, a community, where we could walk together, even if we were apart? A place where people could share, learn, and help others find their way through the darkness?

This book is my journey. It's not polished or pretty, but it's honest. It's the story of a kid who grew up scared of his own home and classmates. A boy who has battled demons ever since and refuses to let them win. I hope that by sharing my *hardest walk,* you'll feel less alone in yours.

My childhood was a living nightmare. Fear was my constant companion—at home, at school, everywhere. It felt like the world had it in for me, even my own family, where I should have felt safe and protected... How could I be so disliked? Why was I always the one who seemed to get picked on? Why did it feel like I didn't belong anywhere?

From as early as junior school, the humiliation began. I'd poo my pants—repeatedly. It wasn't a one-off thing; it was a regular occurrence. And no one was about to let me forget it. The kids at school would laugh, point fingers, and call me names. "Smelly" was the most common one. I was "that kid." The one who smelled, the one who sniffed glue in class, the one who cut his own hair during break because he couldn't stand to be around anyone. I didn't know how to make it stop. I had no idea how to fit in.

Looking back at a time when I must have been no more than eight or nine, memories from that time still haunt me. The taunts, the laughter, the feeling of being so completely alone, even in a crowd of people. The names they called me, the way they would look at me as though I was something disgusting—it never stopped. The shame became a part of me, embedded deep inside. It was as though I had been marked for humiliation, as though I was never going to escape the label they had put on me.

At home, things were no better. He didn't just punish me; he terrified me. If I didn't eat dinner, if I didn't do something exactly right, he'd threaten me.

"If you don't eat that, I'll stab you in the eye with a fork!"

The words are seared into my memory, and the worst part wasn't even the threat—it was what I had come to expect. It was the certainty that something was always about to go wrong.

I remember it so clearly, almost as if it happened only yesterday. There he was, standing by the back gate, his eyes locked on me, unmoving, as I stood there helpless in the park, getting taunted and shoved around by the older kids. I could feel the weight of his stare from across the space between us, but there was no sign of movement, no attempt to step forward or intervene. He just watched, as if it wasn't happening, as though I wasn't there at all. I couldn't understand it. Why didn't he do anything? Didn't he see how much it hurt, how scared I was? His cold, impassive gaze felt like a betrayal — it made the whole thing even worse. To me, it seemed like he could have easily helped me, or at least said something, shouted and frightened my tormentors away, but instead, he just stood there, as though I didn't even matter. The confusion and pain of that moment stayed with me for a long time.

"Smelly" became my identity—reinforced daily by my parents, by my classmates, and even by myself. It was like a shackle that couldn't be broken. I was branded with this name, and no matter how hard I tried to change, no one would let me forget it.

But amidst all this, there was a small flicker of light. One thing that I do remember from an early age was a tall man whom I would occasionally see standing by the back gate, chatting quietly with my mum. I didn't know who he was or what his role was in our lives, but there was something about him—a warmth, a kindness. His big, warm smile stayed with me. It felt like a beacon of hope in a world that seemed to be lacking it.

In a world where cruelty and fear seemed to rule, this man's kindness felt like a small, powerful gesture of hope. It was as though he was a silent guardian, always present in the background of my life. He wasn't always there, but when he was, I felt like, just maybe, I wasn't as alone as I thought I was. It was a small thing, but at that time, it meant everything to me.

My next-door neighbours were another source of light. They were, quite simply, the best people you could ever hope to have as neighbours. They always seemed to sense that something wasn't quite right with me, even though they never said anything directly. They were just... there. They didn't judge me. They didn't push me. But their presence was a comfort.

The lady of the house was a deputy head teacher at the local infant school. She had a calming, nurturing presence that made me feel safe when everything else around me felt like it was falling apart. This was the 1980s, a different era—where emotions weren't discussed openly. It was a time when the "stiff upper lip" was the rule, not the exception. But these people knew something wasn't right. They didn't need to ask. They could just sense it.

Between the ages of eleven and twelve, these wonderful neighbours became my escape. Every summer, they would take me with them on their caravan trips. For the entire six-week school holiday, I was able to experience something I had never known before: safety. For the first time, I felt genuinely cared for.

Looking back, I think they knew how much I needed that. They never asked about my family. They never questioned why I was always so quiet, so distant. They just let me be. But they gave me something priceless: security. Something I hadn't even realised I was missing until I experienced it. Those trips became the best days of my younger life, and I carry the warmth of those memories with me even now.

There are parts of me, fragments really, that I've buried so deep I've come to believe they don't exist. The memories, I mean, from when I was younger. They should have been forgotten long ago, tucked away where no one – not even me – could reach them. But somehow, they linger, hiding in the dark corners of my mind, like shadows that won't shift no matter how much light you shine on them. I can never quite grasp them, but I know they're there, just out of reach, like something you're sure is around the corner, but when you turn, it's gone.

I don't remember everything. In fact, I try not to. There's a part of me that wishes I could forget it all. But the harder I try, the more elusive they become. Faces that should be familiar are blurry. Conversations that should have made sense are nothing but echoes of harsh tones. And yet, every now and then, something will trigger it. A smell, a sound, an old song – and for just a moment, I catch a glimpse of something, a fleeting image, like the tail end of a nightmare slipping away. It's there for a second, and then it's gone again.

But the feelings don't go away so easily. They're harder to escape. The coldness, the isolation. The anger, the confusion. They creep in when I least expect it, just beneath the surface, like the edge of a memory trying to break through. I can feel them, like a weight pressing down on me, pulling me back to something I can't quite remember but know I've lived.

It's as if my mind has protected me from the worst of it, but not without cost. The memories are locked away; hidden behind a door I can't open. And sometimes, I wonder whether I'm better off that way. What would it do to me if I finally uncovered them? Would it tear me apart? Or would it finally set me free?

For now, they stay where they are – in that shadowy place, just beyond my reach. Always there, waiting. And I, I keep moving forward, pretending I don't hear their whispers.

When I wasn't with those angels on earth, I did everything I could to escape my reality. I faked sickness, forged my mum's signature, and when that didn't work, I hid. Once, I spent an entire day crammed inside a black wheely bin just to avoid school. It wasn't about laziness. It wasn't about not wanting to learn—it was about surviving. It was the only way I knew how to protect myself.

My dirty underwear? I'd throw it out or hide it under my bed, only for my parents to find it and unleash even more punishment. The cycle never ended. Fear, shame, punishment—it was like a never-ending storm.

By 15, I couldn't take it anymore. I ran away to a family friend's house, leaving school behind for good. No exams, no closure—just a feeling of overwhelming relief. The weight that had been pressing on my chest for so long seemed to lift, even though I knew I was running from something I couldn't escape so easily.

But the scars of those years? They stayed with me. They carved themselves into my soul, marking me in ways I couldn't fully understand. Those years shaped who I became, and even now, I carry the weight of them. But they didn't define me—not completely. And your past won't define you either.

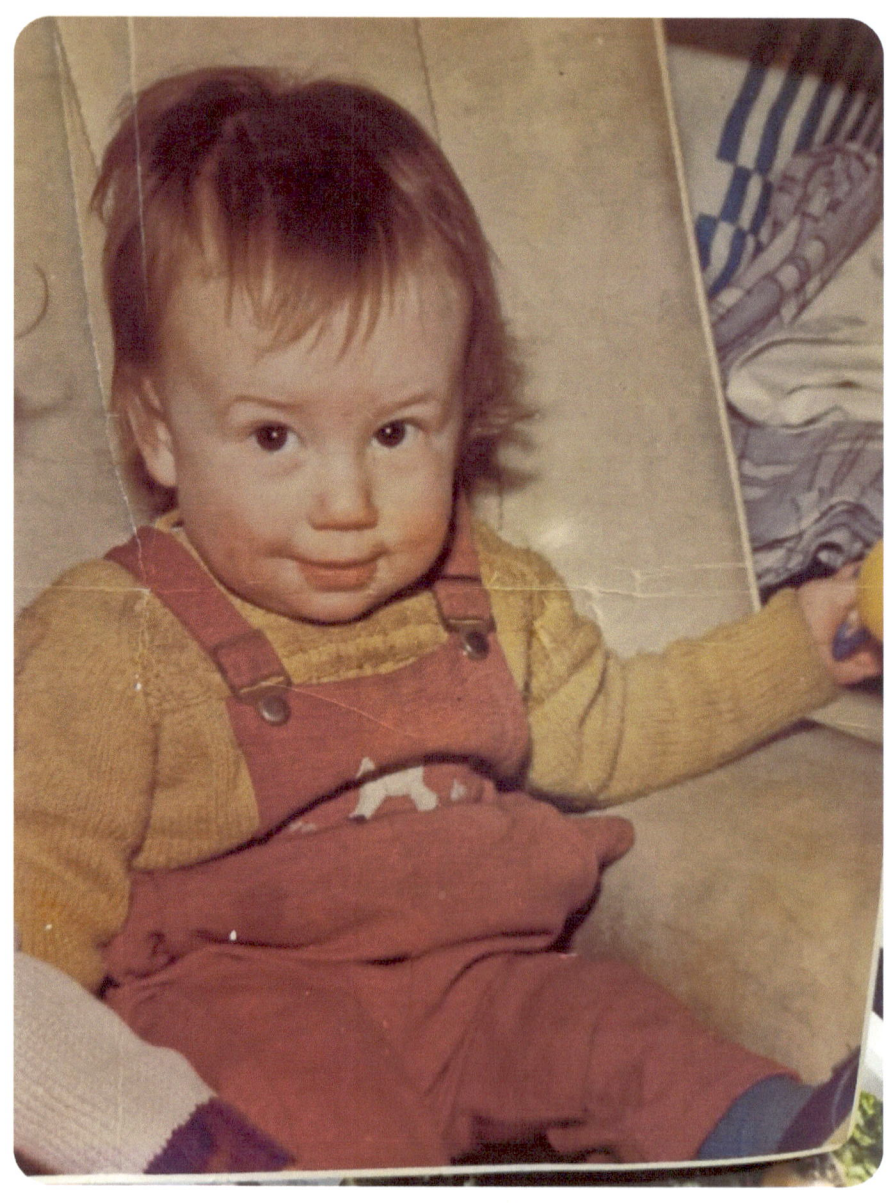

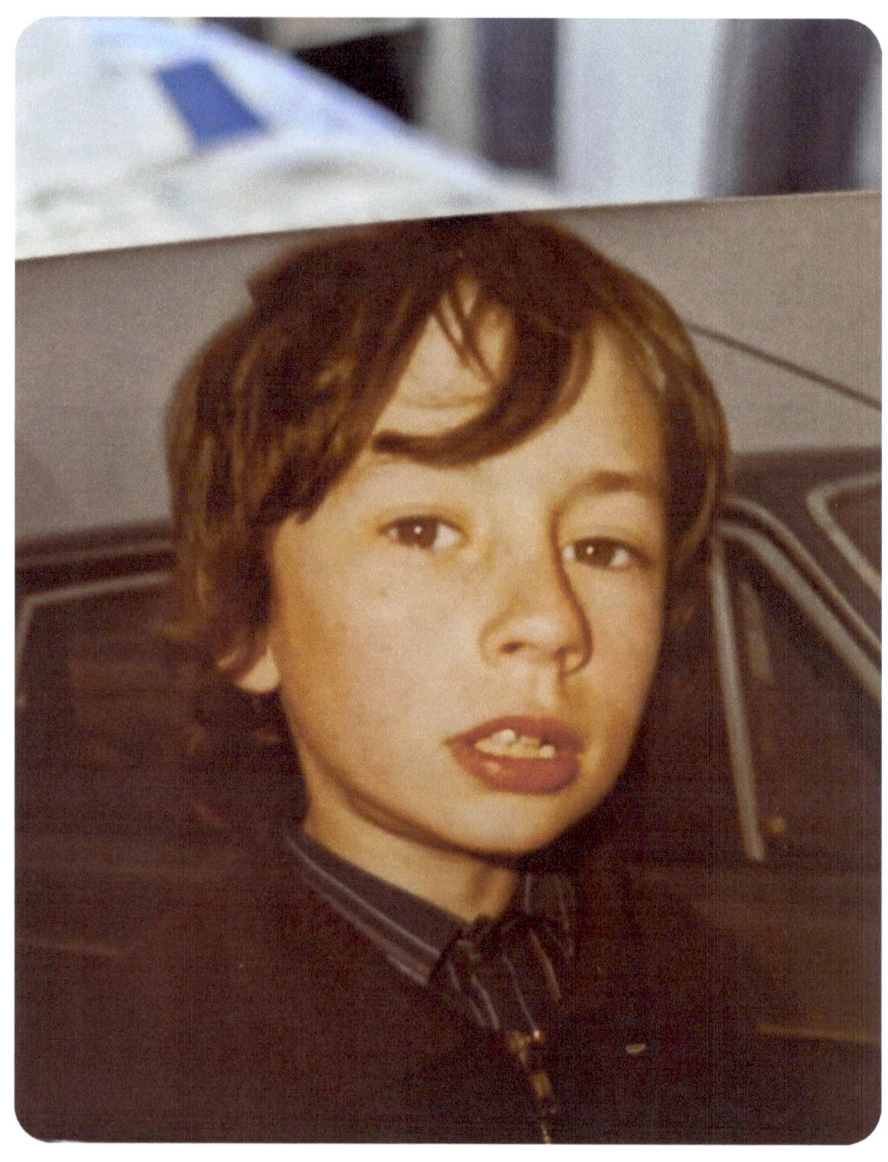

Chapter Two

Fighting to Survive

By the time I was 15 years old, my world felt like it was crumbling around me. Anxiety had taken up permanent residence in my chest, my shyness spiralled into isolation and a heavy cloud of depression hung over my days. It was suffocating. I couldn't breathe without it feeling like something was pressing down on my lungs. Every part of me was consumed by fear. Even looking in the mirror became unbearable—every glance brought the reflection of someone I despised: a smelly, worthless individual who couldn't seem to find his place in the world. I was lost, drowning in a sea of my own self-loathing, trapped and unable to escape.

School, which should have been a place of learning and growth, had become a battleground. The place that was supposed to offer refuge, support, and safety was now the front line of my war against the world. Every day, I braced myself for another onslaught—another round of mockery, teasing, or worse. Toward the end of my time there, a devastating rumour about me began to spread. The kids discovered that I was living with a man who was much older than me—a gay man. You can just imagine the ammunition that gave them.

It was the early 1990s, and being gay at that time wasn't just a label; it was a weapon. Being labelled as gay person was to be steeped in stigma, fear, and ignorance, fuelled even further by the HIV/AIDS crisis. The cruelty of the words they used—"queer," "faggot," "bum boy"—cut deeper than I can tell you, even now. They weren't just words; they were like knives, each one leaving a scar. I felt like an outcast, branded with a shame I didn't deserve, one that followed me wherever I went. What made it worse was that the relationship with this family friend wasn't even romantic or sexual—he was simply someone who took me in when I had nowhere else to go. But that didn't matter to my tormentors. They twisted it, used it as an excuse to make me the target of their cruelty. The pressure mounted daily, suffocating me, until I was nothing more than a shadow of myself, a boy with no voice and no hope.

One day, I remember sitting in class, trying to hold myself together as their words rained down on me. "Look at him," one of the boys whispered to his mate, "living with that old bloke. Weird, isn't it? Must be some sort of freak."

"More like a raving poof!" His friend sniggered.

And they'd all laugh. That laugh, the one that made my insides twist with shame, it felt like it would never stop. I was an easy target, and they knew it. I wished I could disappear, wished the ground would swallow me whole. The cruel comments echoed in my mind long after school had finished. The days blurred together, each one feeling like an endless cycle of dread, anxiety, and humiliation.

Desperate for relief, I went to see a doctor. I didn't know what else to do. I just needed to tell someone how I was feeling, how suffocated I felt by the weight of it all. I tried to explain: "I feel… lost. Everything feels like it's closing in. I can't breathe."

The doctor nodded sympathetically and wrote something down in his notes. "You're experiencing anxiety and depression," he said, like it was a simple diagnosis, as if those words alone could fix me. "I'll prescribe you something to help with your low mood. It's called citalopram. It'll help lift the fog."

I was sceptical, but I took the prescription. I started on 20mg, and at first, I felt nothing. No relief. No change. Just a strange sensation in my body that I couldn't quite place. It made me drowsy, more emotional, and constantly on edge. It wasn't what I expected. It wasn't like the doctor had promised. "It'll take time," he said when I returned to ask why I felt so strange. "It takes time to feel better." But as the months dragged on, my fear and anxiety only grew. The pills weren't helping. They were only masking the real problem, pushing it down but never quite getting rid of it. I couldn't understand why I felt worse when I was supposed to be feeling better.

My life, which had never really been simple or easy, seemed to get even more complicated as I grew older. The cracks began to show in ways I struggled to control or even understand. From the ages of 15 to 17, I lived with a deep, hidden shame that was both isolating and excruciating. I would still find myself soiling my pants—a hangover from my miserable childhood that stayed with me far longer than it should have.

One day, I remember vividly, I was in the school hallway when I felt the cramps start. I tried to ignore them, hoping it would pass, but it only got worse. The pain was unbearable. I collapsed onto the floor, doubled over, and felt the familiar warmth spread in my pants. I was terrified, embarrassed. A friend saw me and rushed over; their face filled with concern.

"Mate, you, okay?" he asked, helping me to my feet.

I could barely speak, my mind in a blur of panic. "I... I don't think I can move..."

Within minutes, I was in an ambulance, rushed to the hospital. The doctors ran tests, did scans, and after what felt like hours, they concluded. "You've got severe irritable bowel syndrome," they said. "It's been aggravated by stress. This has been going on far longer than it should have."

At the hospital, they performed an enema because I hadn't been able to go to the toilet for three weeks. The pain was excruciating. As the doctors worked, they reassured me, telling me it wasn't my fault. But the shame lingered. I could feel the tears welling up, burning my eyes, not from the physical pain but from the humiliation. It wasn't just a medical procedure—it felt like another invasion, another reminder that I was broken in ways I couldn't control.

In that sterile hospital room, I became aware of something else too—how deeply alone I felt. No one else could feel the weight of what I was going through. Not even the doctors, kind as they were. They tried to reassure me, but I couldn't shake the feeling that I was a freak, that something was fundamentally wrong with me. I withdrew even more, my social anxieties deepening. I became even more painfully shy than before.

It was a different time back then. There were no smartphones, no social media, no technology to connect to or to distract me from my pain. I was left alone with my thoughts, isolated in a way that feels unimaginable today. The loneliness was crushing. Every day felt like facing a mountain I didn't have the strength to climb. I wanted to scream, but I had no words, no voice. I was a ghost in my own life.

Things started to change when I turned 16. That same family friend who had been my refuge—who had stepped in when I had nowhere else to go—offered me something unexpected: an opportunity. He helped me get my first job in the engineering industry; a world I knew nothing about but quickly grew to love.

At first, I felt like I was stumbling in the dark, unsure of how I was going to fit in. Would I be any good? What if I failed? But to my surprise, I found my footing faster than I ever expected. I discovered I had a knack for learning new skills. I was eager to prove myself—and I did!

I was welding parts for Triumph motorbike frames, piecing together the intricate components that would make these machines come alive. The pride I felt was indescribable. I had gone from being a frightened boy, hiding in fear, to being someone who could contribute to something tangible, something real. I even worked on parts for a rollercoaster that was bound for Disneyland Paris, set to open in 1992. The idea that I, a 16-year-old kid who had once been paralysed by fear and self-doubt, was helping create something so special—it was surreal. I was good at it. No, I was more than good at it. I was proud of what I did.

And there was another plus—the pay wasn't bad either! On piece-rate work, I was earning £400 a week. For a 16-year-old in the early 90s, that was an absolute fortune. It felt like a dream come true. That money gave me a taste of independence, something I had never had before. For the first time in my life, I felt like I wasn't completely worthless. Just maybe, I did have a future. A future I could shape.

Working in engineering taught me more than just technical skills. It showed me that I could overcome challenges, that I could adapt and thrive in a world that had once felt so hostile. Slowly but surely, I began to rebuild my confidence. Each weld, each project, and each pay slip - all were a step toward a future I could embrace with confidence.

Though the scars of those earlier years remain, I can now honestly say that they no longer define me. Looking back, I see a boy who endured more than any boy or child should have had to. A boy who found a way to keep going, even when the entire world seemed against him. And now, as I write this, I can feel a sense of pride in the journey I've been on. It's been tough, but it's been worth it. I can look in that mirror now and be proud of the man looking back at me.

The journey isn't over. It never truly ends, but I can look back now, not with regret, but with a sense of accomplishment. Because I made it through, and I'm still here. And for that, I'm proud.

Chapter Three

Taking on Giants

Just as I turned 18, life threw me another devastating blow—one that would leave both physical and emotional scars that I still carry to this day. It was a moment of ignorance, one I couldn't have predicted, yet it would change my life forever. I was working on a piece of machinery called a pillar drill—a massive, industrial tool that required proper safety measures and training to operate safely, neither of which I'd been given. It was only my second week on the job, and although I was eager to prove myself, I was still a novice, struggling to catch up with everything I had yet to learn.

That day, I was assigned a task that I should never have been left to do alone. The safety guard on the drill wasn't in place, but I didn't know that it was supposed to be. I had been given thick cotton gloves to protect my hands from metal swarf—standard safety gear, I thought—but I had no idea how dangerous that combination could be.

I brushed the swarf off the workpiece, my mind focused on finishing the job, thinking only of the noise of the drill, the buzz of the machinery. It was an industrial world, after all. A world where speed and efficiency were the order of the day. But in a flash, my right index finger got caught in the spinning drill. I didn't know what was happening until the machine suddenly pulled me in. The force was so strong, I couldn't even comprehend it at first. The drill turned, and my body spun with it, helpless in its grip.

"STOP!" I screamed, my voice cutting through the deafening noise. But the machine kept turning, dragging me further in. My arm twisted horribly, and my body contorted as I was sucked into the mechanism.

"Help! Somebody! Help me!" I screamed again, but my voice was drowned by the sounds of the industrial noise, the gears, and pulleys.

My mind was spinning, the world moving in slow motion. I felt the raw agony in my arm as it snapped, the bone splintering, a sickening crunch that reverberated in my ears. Everything seemed to blur—the horror, the pain, the desperation. Finally, someone hit the emergency stop button, and the machine ground to a halt. But it was too late. I was still caught in the drill. My arm was bent at an unnatural angle, and I felt the hot, sickening wetness of blood soaking through my sleeve.

"Jesus Christ are you alright?" someone shouted. I looked up, but everything was blurred through the pain.

Someone was there, pulling me away from the machine, but I could barely comprehend what was happening. The agony in my arm was unbearable, and I felt light-headed, dizzy from the shock. I don't know how long I lay there, but the ambulance arrived soon enough, and I was rushed to the hospital. Doses of gas and air were pumped into my system to dull the burning, searing pain from my mangled arm.

I spent the next two weeks in the hospital, confined to a sterile bed, my body recovering from the trauma. The surgeries were gruelling. The doctors inserted metal plates into my arm, attempting to piece me back together. But the scar that would remain—both physical and emotional—was something that no doctor could fix.

While I was recovering, a health and safety representative came to see me. He seemed genuine enough, but I couldn't help but feel a sense of dread when he spoke.

"We're launching an investigation into the company," he told me quietly.

"This should never have happened. They'll be held accountable."

I wanted to believe him, but the reality was far different. A week later, I discovered that my accident had made the national news. The Daily Mirror, of all papers, carried the headline:

"A Horrific Industrial Accident."

It wasn't the kind of attention I wanted. Suddenly, my nightmare had been plastered across the pages of a newspaper, and all I wanted was to forget it.

But instead of taking responsibility, the company turned on me. I was blindsided when I found out they had launched an attack on my character. They accused me of lying, claiming that I had been professionally trained and that it was my fault I had sustained the injuries. The betrayal cut deeper than anything else. I felt like the ground had been pulled from under me. This wasn't just an injury—it was a fight for my very dignity.

"They're saying you were properly trained," one of my coworkers told me, shaking his head. "I don't know how they can say that. You weren't. None of us were. It's a bloody joke!"

But the nightmare didn't end there. I was plagued with vivid, terrifying nightmares, reliving the moment when I was dragged into the machine. I would wake drenched in sweat, my heart pounding, my body shaking. I could still hear the whirring of the drill, still feel the pain as if it was happening repeatedly. I developed Post-Traumatic Stress Disorder (PTSD), and every time I heard the sound of heavy machinery or saw a similar piece of equipment, I would spiral into a panic attack. The days were long, and the nights were even longer.

Post-Traumatic Stress Disorder (PTSD) *is a mental health condition that can develop after an individual has experienced or witnessed a traumatic event.*

Causes and Risk Factors

PTSD can develop after any event that overwhelms an individual's ability to cope, such as:

- ***Combat Exposure****: Soldiers or veterans are often exposed to combat situations that can lead to PTSD.*
- ***Physical or Sexual Assault****: People who have been victims of violence, including domestic abuse, sexual assault, or robbery, are at higher risk.*
- ***Natural Disasters or Accidents****: Survivors of hurricanes, earthquakes, car accidents, or plane crashes may develop PTSD.*
- ***Sudden Loss****: A traumatic death or witnessing a loved one's suffering can also trigger PTSD, especially if the loss was violent or sudden.*

Certain factors can increase the risk of developing PTSD, including:

- ***History of Trauma****: People with a previous history of trauma, such as childhood abuse or neglect, are more likely to develop PTSD.*
- ***Lack of Support****: A lack of social support following a traumatic event can make it harder to process the trauma and recover.*
- ***Previous Mental Health Issues****: Individuals with pre-existing mental health conditions, such as depression or anxiety, are at greater risk of developing PTSD.*

- ***The Severity of the Trauma***: *The more intense and prolonged the trauma, the higher the likelihood of developing PTSD.*

Symptoms of PTSD

PTSD is characterized by several key symptoms, often grouped into four main categories:

1. ***Intrusive Memories***:
   - ***Flashbacks***: *Individuals with PTSD may relive the traumatic event through vivid flashbacks or nightmares, often feeling as though they are experiencing the trauma again in real time.*
   - ***Distressing Memories***: *Persistent, unwanted thoughts or memories of the event may flood the individual's mind, creating feelings of anxiety and fear.*
   - ***Nightmares***: *Nightmares related to the traumatic experience are common, causing sleep disturbances and increasing stress.*

2. ***Avoidance***:
   - ***Avoiding reminders***: *Individuals may go to great lengths to avoid situations, places, or people that remind them of the trauma. This can include avoiding certain locations, conversations, or even topics that bring up memories of the event.*
   - ***Emotional numbness***: *People with PTSD may withdraw from relationships and feel emotionally numb or detached, finding it difficult to experience joy or connect with others. This may result in isolation and a sense of being emotionally "disconnected."*

3. ***Negative Changes in Thoughts and Mood***:
   - ***Negative Beliefs***: *Individuals with PTSD often develop distorted or negative beliefs about themselves or others. They might feel guilt or shame, believing that they are somehow responsible for the trauma, or they may feel like the world is unsafe.*
   - ***Hopelessness***: *They might experience feelings of hopelessness or despair about the future and feel that life will never return to normal.*
   - ***Difficulty in relationships***: *People with PTSD often struggle to trust others, leading to difficulty in maintaining close or supportive relationships.*

- ***Emotional Reactions****:* They may experience extreme emotional reactions, including irritability, anger, or rage. These reactions may seem disproportionate to the situation and can affect their personal and professional lives.

4. ***Increased Arousal Symptoms****:*
   - ***Hypervigilance****:* Individuals with PTSD are often on edge, constantly feeling alert or "on guard" for danger, even in safe environments. This can cause them to startle easily, remain excessively watchful, or feel like something bad is about to happen.
   - ***Sleep disturbances****:* Difficulty falling or staying asleep is common, and nightmares can exacerbate this. Lack of proper rest contributes to fatigue and irritability.
   - ***Concentration Problems****:* Difficulty concentrating on tasks or remembering details due to constant distraction by intrusive thoughts or emotional overload.
   - ***Self-destructive Behaviours****:* Some individuals may engage in reckless or harmful behaviours like substance abuse or risky activities to cope with the distressing feelings.

Diagnosis

A diagnosis of PTSD is typically made by a mental health professional, such as a psychologist or psychiatrist, based on the individual's reported symptoms. To be diagnosed, the individual must have experienced symptoms for at least one month following the trauma, and these symptoms must significantly impair daily functioning.

Treatment

The treatment for PTSD often involves a combination of therapy and medication, tailored to the individual's needs. Common forms of treatment include:

1. ***Psychotherapy****:*
   - ***Cognitive Behavioural Therapy (CBT)****:* One of the most effective forms of therapy for PTSD. CBT helps individuals understand the relationship between thoughts, feelings, and behaviours, and work on

changing the negative thought patterns that contribute to the trauma response.
- **Exposure Therapy**: A type of CBT that involves safely exposing the individual to memories or situations related to the trauma in a controlled environment, helping them process the memories and reduce their distress over time.
- **Eye Movement Desensitization and Reprocessing (EMDR)**: This therapy uses eye movements to help the brain process traumatic memories, reducing their emotional charge.

2. **Medication**:
   - **Antidepressants**: Medications such as SSRIs (selective serotonin reuptake inhibitors) or SNRIs (serotonin-norepinephrine reuptake inhibitors) are often prescribed to help manage the mood and anxiety symptoms of PTSD.
   - **Anti-anxiety Medication**: Short-term use of anti-anxiety medications can help manage the symptoms, but they are generally not a long-term solution.
   - **Prazosin**: This medication may be prescribed to help reduce nightmares associated with PTSD.

3. **Self-Care and Support**:
   - **Support Groups**: Joining support groups or community programs, such as those provided by mental health charities, can provide a sense of connection and understanding.
   - **Mindfulness and Relaxation**: Techniques such as meditation, yoga, and deep breathing exercises can help manage stress and reduce anxiety.
   - **Lifestyle Changes**: Regular exercise, a healthy diet, and adequate sleep are important for managing PTSD symptoms and promoting overall mental health.

Impact on Life

Untreated PTSD can affect every area of a person's life. Relationships often suffer due to difficulty with trust and emotional numbing. Work performance may decline because of concentration problems, irritability, and absenteeism due to poor mental health. People with PTSD may also engage in unhealthy coping mechanisms, such as substance abuse, to numb their emotions.

However, with the right treatment, recovery from PTSD is possible. It may take time, but many individuals find that with therapy, support, and lifestyle changes, they can regain control over their lives and significantly reduce the impact of PTSD on their daily functioning.

It's important to recognise that PTSD is not a sign of weakness. It is a natural, human response to trauma, and seeking help is a brave and crucial step in the healing process.

For the next four years, I fought tirelessly to clear my name. With the help of a solicitor, I sought compensation for the physical and emotional trauma that I had endured. It was an uphill battle against a massive company with all the resources at its disposal. They had their lawyers, their PR machine, their money, and their power. They seemed determined to crush me, to make me disappear, to make it all my fault. But despite their efforts, I refused to give up.

In one meeting, a senior representative from the company looked at me, a cold, calculating look in his eyes. "This is a minor issue," he said dismissively. "We don't need to waste more time on it. You should be thankful we're offering anything at all."

I clenched my fists, my blood boiling. I wanted to scream, to let lose all the frustration and anger I had bottled up. But I kept quiet. I had to. I had to stay strong for myself. I had to show them that I wouldn't back down.

Finally, after years of legal battles, endless meetings, and sleepless nights, I won the case. The company admitted their negligence and liability. They settled out of court, offering me a substantial sum. Not long after, the company went bankrupt. It was a hollow victory. I should have felt relief, but I didn't. It wasn't over. The nightmares still haunted me, and no amount of money could erase the memories.

The victory should have felt like closure, but instead, it felt like more of a beginning—one that I hadn't expected. The legal battle was over, but the real fight had just begun. The trauma from that day would live with me forever. I wasn't just recovering from physical injuries; I was recovering from the emotional wreckage of betrayal, fear, and loss.

Even now, those years of pain and struggle linger like lurking demons in my mind. The scars may have healed, but the emotional weight still hangs over me. I'm no longer the same person I was before the accident. I carry those memories with me every day—memories of a broken body, broken trust, and the long, hard road to recovery.

But through it all, I've learned that survival isn't about overcoming physical wounds—it's about facing the emotional scars and finding strength in the darkest moments. Today, the scars, both seen and unseen, linger. Yet, amidst the darkness, I've discovered resilience. Survival isn't merely about enduring and surviving physical wounds; it's about confronting emotional turmoil head-on and finding strength in the depths of adversity. That, more than anything else, has become my greatest victory.

PILLAR DRILL THAT WAS VERY SIMILAR TO THE ONE THAT PULLED ME IN

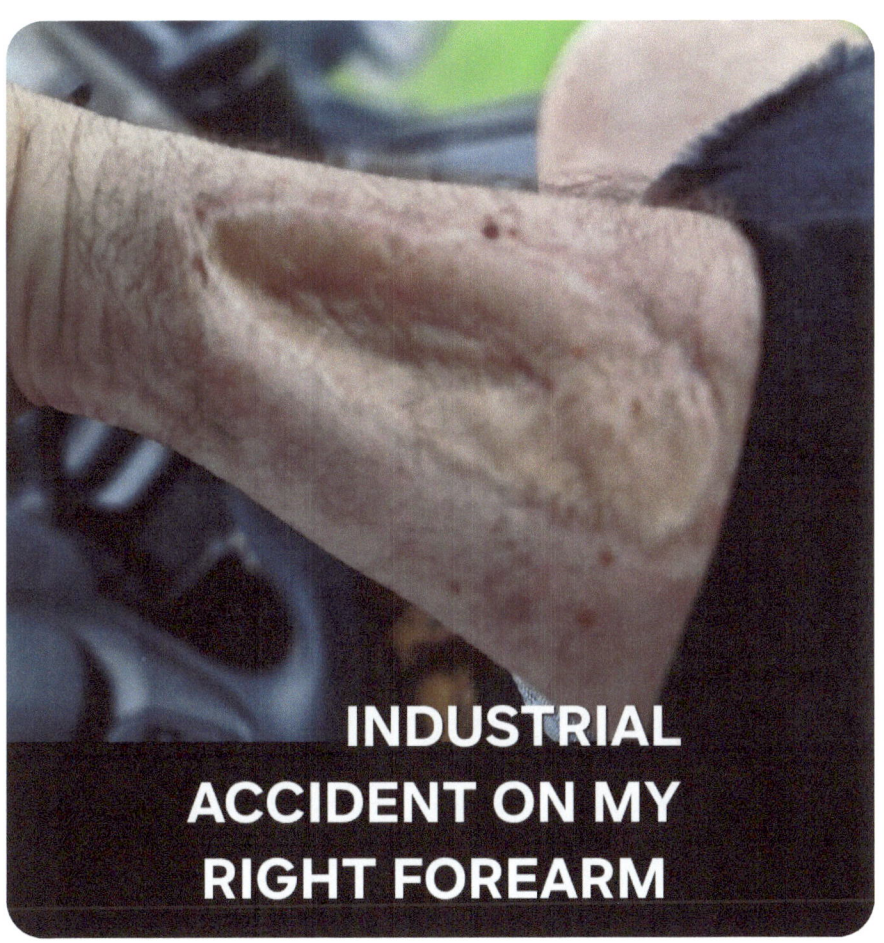

Chapter Four

Betrayal

By the time I turned 21, it felt like my entire world had collapsed in on itself. The weight of it all pressed down on me, suffocating any hope that had once been there. Four years had passed since the accident, and those years had been a relentless storm of trauma and turmoil, each day dragging me further into a spiral of confusion and despair. The night of the accident still haunted me, its aftermath of lies and courtroom battles left me utterly shattered. It felt like I was stuck in a nightmare that I could never escape, my reality warped by the trauma I'd been through. The company had betrayed me, and in the end, so had the people I had trusted most.

"I can't do this anymore," I confessed to my counsellor one evening, my voice trembling under the weight of my own despair. The words felt like they were being torn out of me. "The medications—the citalopram, the sertraline—they were supposed to help, but they just make everything foggy. I feel like I'm drowning." I stared at my hands, clasped tightly in my lap, as if I could somehow hold myself together by sheer force of will.

My counsellor, an older man with a kind face, nodded thoughtfully, his eyes filled with a quiet understanding. "The meds take time to work, but you're clearly going through something much deeper. We need to find ways to navigate this, step by step."

But it was hard to hear him. I couldn't make sense of anything anymore. My life felt like a jumble of broken pieces that I couldn't fit back together. My only solace came in fleeting moments, often drowned in alcohol and drugs, desperate attempts to numb the overwhelming pain that threatened to consume me. I thought that if I just drank enough or took enough pills, I could make it all go away, even if it was only for a short while. Each sip, each pill, promised relief but only dragged me deeper into darkness. The cycle was vicious, and I couldn't seem to break free.

Amidst this chaos, there was one constant. My gay friend—he had always been there for me, a rock in my stormy sea. He was the one person who never judged me, who never made me feel like I was less than human. We shared a bond forged through trials and tribulations, both of us battered by life's cruel hands. As I bounced from job to job, searching for purpose in a haze of despair, he remained by my side.

It wasn't until much later that I found my thing—building septic tanks. The work wasn't glamorous, not by any stretch of the imagination, but it grounded me. It was simple, dirty work, but it gave me something to focus on, something to hold onto. The endless hours spent outside, digging, welding, and assembling, provided a rare sense of control amidst the chaos of my life. The long hours of night shifts became my sanctuary. I could lose myself in the rhythm of the job, and for a brief time, the weight on my chest would lift. I finally felt a semblance of stability, even if only temporarily, while the rest of my life seemed to teeter on the brink.

During this time, my relationship with "Little Nan," my father's mother, grew stronger. She had always been a petite, gentle soul—someone whose love felt like a warm blanket in the coldest of times. As her health declined, we decided, my friend and I: we would move in with her, taking care of her in her final days. It wasn't just an act of kindness; it was an honour and a privilege. She had given me so much love over the years, and now it was our turn to repay that kindness, to be there for her when she needed us most.

But just as life seemed to settle, tragedy struck again. Little Nan passed away, and her death unleashed a cascade of events that would test my resilience to its limits. He, already entangled in his own complicated life, suddenly left my mother, blaming her for everything. I couldn't understand it—he was supposed to be there for her, to support her as her health deteriorated, but instead, he turned his back, oblivious to the fact that my mother was struggling with her own mental health issues.

"I can't do this alone," my voice cracked one evening as I confided in my counsellor. "She's falling apart, and I'm barely holding on myself. What can I do? I'm not strong enough for this. I'm so tired." The tears welled up in my eyes as I spoke. The weight of the responsibility was overwhelming, and I didn't know where to turn. His departure had left us both reeling. I could feel my mother's pain, but I was too broken to be the support she needed.

With Little Nan gone, the house became a battleground. Despite our verbal agreement with her that we could live there rent-free in exchange for caretaking, his sisters contested our right to be there. They claimed we were squatting and pushed us into a legal battle I never saw coming. Standing in that courtroom, I felt small and insignificant as the judge's words landed with crushing weight. "Can you pay?" he asked, his voice stern, cold. "What will you pay a week?"

My voice trembled, barely audible. The words seemed to fall out of my mouth in a hopeless whisper. "Five pounds a month…"

The judge's disdainful gaze crushed me even further. Each syllable of his scathing condemnation cut deeper than the last, his words echoing in my mind long after I left the courtroom. The system, it seemed, was set against me. The years of struggle, of fighting for my dignity, had led me here—nowhere. Outside the courtroom, I unravelled completely. The pain, the injustice, the sheer betrayal- it was all too much. I sought solace in the familiar numbness of substances. I drowned my despair in alcohol, drugs, anything that could push the sharp edges of reality away, even for a brief moment.

"My friend…" I choke on the words; the pain of betrayal is still raw. "He didn't even try to help. We drifted apart, and he faded away, leaving me to face the nightmare, alone." The friendship that had once meant the world to me had crumbled, disappearing into the ether, just when I needed it most.

While he and his sisters fought over their inheritance, moving on with their lives, I returned to the home I had fled years before. It was now a refuge for my broken mother,

I remember one Christmas Day, as I was preparing dinner for mum and me, I tried to make it feel normal, even though everything in me screamed that nothing was normal anymore. I wanted to give my mother something to hold onto, something to bring a semblance of joy into our broken lives. But as I was setting the table, trying to make everything right, there was a knock at the door.

I opened it, wondering who it could be, but when I saw who was standing there, my heart dropped. It was him. He was wanting a divorce on Christmas day. On Christmas Day, of all days.

The pain was searing. It was a betrayal that cut deeper than any courtroom judgment. He the man who should have been a source of strength, had turned his back on us in our most vulnerable moment. He had destroyed what little was left of my family, and he didn't even have the decency to wait until after Christmas.

In 2013, I finally saw him again after years apart. I had so many questions, and I just wanted him to be honest with me about everything, to explain why I felt so hated. I thought maybe he had changed, that all I needed was for him to admit what happened and say sorry. My mum had apologised and done what she could to make up for it, and I had forgiven her. She had her own struggles, things that weren't really her fault.

Later in my life, when he met my fiancée, Deb, I thought things might finally be OK. But, as I've come to realise since then, I was wrong.

But amidst the darkness, there were glimmers of light. My auntie, the one who was like a sister I never had, stood there with my grandad. He was the tall figure I had spoken of so often—the one who had always been my hero. They had come to help protect my mum, to shield my mum from further harm. I can't explain the depth of emotion that overcame me as I recall that moment. The sense of relief, of safety, flooded through me, and I felt tears prick at my eyes. I couldn't hold them back as I looked at my auntie and grandad.

"They're here," I said, "they're here to help."

That Christmas, my auntie and grandad really came to the rescue. They moved him out of the house, getting him away from mum. They protected mum in the way she so desperately needed. But still, Christmas was ruined. Stolen from us once again by his thoughtlessness. When Grandad died years later, it hit me hard. This man had been my saviour and although we had not seen each other very frequently, it felt like my last support had been knocked away.

In that moment, I realised something. Despite everything that had been taken from us, we still had each other. We were still standing. And that, in the end, was what mattered.

As I write these words, tears prick my eyes. But there's a point in sharing this story. It's a journey through pain, yes, but also a testament to resilience. A story of finding hope amidst shattered dreams. And through it all, I hope more than anything that sharing my story might bring healing—not just to me, but to others who have walked their own hard walk.

Chapter Five

Moving On

They say time is a healer, but after two or three years, I was still drowning. The clock moved forward, but I couldn't escape the dark currents that kept threatening to pull me under. Every day felt like a huge struggle, a battle I couldn't win. I'd go to work and do what was expected of me, but inside, I was falling apart, piece by piece. The world kept moving around me, but I was trapped in a haze, stuck in my own head, unable to break free from the weight of it all.

I was drinking myself senseless on top of the antidepressants. The alcohol would blur the edges of everything, giving me temporary relief, while the pills kept me numb enough to get through the day. It was a delicate balance—one I could barely keep up. I couldn't feel anything. Not properly, at least. That numbness became my refuge, my only escape from the chaos inside my head. I didn't want to feel. I didn't want to think. I just wanted to survive the day.

I about managed to hold down a job. I clung to that because it was the only thing I could rely on, the only thing that kept me from spiralling completely. But even that was starting to slip away from me. The weekends were a blur of binge drinking, trying to forget, trying to numb the reality of my life. I'd go out with no intention other than to lose myself, to forget everything for a few hours. I'd hit the clubs, down drink after drink, and try to pick someone up. Anyone. It didn't matter who. I'd end up with some random girl, in some random bed, trying desperately to find comfort in the warmth of another body. But it never worked. It never filled the emptiness inside me.

It was a pattern—one-night stands, meaningless connections. I'd wake up the next morning, feeling worse than before, and stare at myself in the mirror. "Who are you?" I'd ask the reflection staring back at me. "This isn't you." But the words were empty, hollow. The loneliness was suffocating. I was a shell of myself, just going through the motions, existing but not really living.

I wanted to scream. I wanted to rip everything apart, but I didn't know how. "This isn't you!" I kept telling myself, as if repeating the words would make them true. But they never did. I couldn't escape the feeling that I was lost, adrift in a world that didn't care. The weight of everything pressing down on me, day after day. I'd sit in my room at night, staring at the ceiling, the silence unbearable. The stillness of the house felt like it was crushing me. There were no answers, no solutions, just a deep sense of despair.

A couple of years passed. I moved from one job to the next, but I never felt settled. I'd show up, try to act normal, but inside, the paranoia was eating me alive. Every time someone looked at me, I felt like they could see right through me, that they knew something was wrong. They must know. They must see it! I'd second-guess every conversation, every glance. It was exhausting. I didn't trust anyone—not even myself.

I found myself back at my mum's house, the place I swore I'd never return to. It felt like the ultimate defeat. I hated being there, but it was all I had left. The house felt like a cage, the walls suffocating, reminding me of everything I was running away from. But there she was—my mum, struggling too. Her mental health was deteriorating, and she needed me. But I was too broken to help her. I could barely keep myself together, let alone anyone else.

"Are you okay?" she'd ask, her voice cracked with worry, her concern evident in her eyes.

I'd smile, telling her everything was fine, even though I knew it wasn't. "I'm fine, Mum. Really." But the words felt like lies. I wanted to help her, I did, but how could I help anyone when I was barely holding myself together? The house was full of regrets and unspoken words. We were both sinking, and the weight of it all was too much. It felt like we were both trapped in our own personal hells, each too scared to reach out to the other.

By the time I hit 31, I had nothing left. My reputation in town had taken a hit—people whispered behind my back about my reckless behaviour, my failed relationships, the drinking. It felt like I was constantly under a microscope, being judged for everything I had done and everything I had failed to do. But to be honest, it didn't matter anymore. I was numb to it all. I was beyond caring. I wanted out. I needed to get away from the shame, from the memories, from the life I had built that felt like a prison. I didn't care where I went—I just needed to leave.

Then, in October 2007, Mum made the decision to sell the house. She wanted to start fresh, to leave behind the past that had defined her for so long. And I saw it—my chance. My moment to escape, to break free from everything that had kept me chained for so long.

"Where are you going?" Mum asked one night, her voice shaking as she held out an envelope. I took it from her, not sure what to expect. It contained a cheque—the proceeds from the sale of the house—along with a note. Her handwriting was shaky, but the words hit me like a punch to the gut.

"I just want you to be happy. I feel like I've failed you, but I love you. I always will."

Mum told me so many things over the years, she answered all the questions I asked, patiently explaining everything as best as she could. But there was one thing I never understood. Even though I was growing up, and everyone around me seemed to change and mature, I never once saw Mum wear makeup. Not once. I kept asking her why, and eventually, she told me the truth. She said it was because he had told her she couldn't wear it. At first, I didn't really get what that meant, but then she told me something that hit me like a punch to the gut. She said that he had told her that if she left him, he would kill her. I couldn't believe it at first — how could someone say something like that to someone they loved? To my mum? It didn't make sense. The thought of it made my chest tighten and my stomach twist with a mix of anger and confusion. It felt like the world I thought I knew was suddenly shattered, and I didn't know who to trust or what to feel anymore.

The guilt in her words crushed me. I felt the weight of it all, the unspoken ache in her heart that she couldn't fix me. She couldn't make me whole again. And I'd never told her how much I loved her—not like this. Not with the weight of everything we'd been through. I swallowed the lump in my throat, the tears threatening to spill.

"I love you too, Mum," I whispered, the words barely escaping my lips. But it wasn't enough. It never would be. The weight of everything—of all that had been lost—hung heavy between us.

I looked at the road atlas, flicked through the pages, and then, with my eyes closed, I stabbed at it with my finger. Wherever my finger landed, that was where I was going. When I opened my eyes, I looked down at the page. Underneath my finger was the city of Bath. The decision was made.

I drove away without looking back. I couldn't. If I did, I might never leave.

The drive was long, my mind racing with thoughts I couldn't quiet. I had no plan, no clue what I was doing. My finger had landed on Bath City on the map, but I didn't even know what to expect. I didn't care. I just had to get out. I remember the first night I arrived, sitting in my car, exhausted, staring at the unfamiliar streets of Bath. The magnificent Georgian architecture was completely lost on me. All I could feel was the pounding of my heart, the uncertainty of everything. I didn't know anyone here. I didn't know what I was walking into. But I couldn't turn back. I knew that. It wasn't an option.

I quickly found a place to live; a house share in a Victorian house. There were eight other people living there, strangers to me, and it was a strange feeling. I felt like an outsider, an intruder in their world. At first, I didn't know how to fit in. It was like being in a fishbowl, everyone watching but no one really seeing me. Slowly, though, I started getting used to it. I found my rhythm. I started feeling a bit more like me, little by little.

I registered with a doctor right away. The meds were still a part of my life, and I knew I couldn't afford to mess that up. I had been on antidepressants for years—first citalopram, then sertraline. I couldn't afford any mistakes with my meds. I had enough problems already.

I was also battling what they now call health anxiety but back then they called it hypochondria. If something hurt, I'd panic. If I felt off, I'd run to the doctor. If any rare disease or condition was mentioned on television, I was sure I had it. I hated myself for it, but it was a part of me I couldn't shake.

"You're okay," the doctor reassured me when I explained my fears. "We'll keep an eye on things."

But I couldn't let go. I still felt like something was wrong with me, but I kept going. I kept fighting.

I registered with a work agency, and within days, I had landed a temporary role at an engineering firm. It wasn't much, but it was something. For the first time in a long time, I felt like I was getting my footing back.

The first few weeks in Bath were tough, but each day got a little easier. I started making connections with people who didn't know me. They didn't know my past, and that was a relief. Bath became my second chance. It was messy, but it was mine. And for the first time in years, I felt like I was starting to live again.

Chapter Six

My Journey Continues...–

Two years had passed, and at last, my life was finally starting to settle. The storm, although not completely over, seemed to calm down just enough to let me catch my breath. I had been told that I now had a permanent job, and that was a huge positive for me—a milestone that felt monumental, especially considering my history of instability. A stable job—something I hadn't had in the past—was a small victory. I felt like I had finally found some solid ground to stand on, even if the ground beneath me still seemed fragile at times.

But behind the scenes, the battle inside was far from over. I was fighting an internal war that no one could see, a battle I was losing more often than I was winning. On the surface, I looked fine. I kept a straight face, kept moving, kept pretending. I'd put on a brave face at work. I had to. I couldn't afford to be the weak link. And I think I did a decent job of it. But when I was in the quiet of my house share, the façade would start to crack, and everything would come crashing down.

The silence in my room was deafening. It swallowed me whole, pulling me back into the dark recesses of my mind. I was not a "people person." I had always been shy, vulnerable even, and that wasn't something I could just switch off. No matter how much I tried to convince myself that I was fine, the cracks were starting to show. It was like being on stage, pretending to be someone I wasn't, while my real self was crumbling behind the scenes. I kept telling myself, *just fake it till you make it*, but those words lost their power after a while. They stopped making sense. I felt like I was lying to everyone— my coworkers, my friends, and most of all, myself.

There were nights when I'd curl up in bed, the weight of everything pressing on me, the tears coming when I least expected them. It felt like there was no escape. I'd close my eyes and pray, *please, demons, leave me alone. Let me just live. Let me breathe without the fear of falling apart.* But the fear never let go. It kept clawing at me, pulling me deeper into the darkness.

The new doctor I'd seen put me on a different antidepressant. This was the third different one since I'd started on them when I was 15. Duloxetine. They gave me the highest dose they could give me. Along with that, I had diazepam to calm my nerves if needed. I hated relying on medication, but it was the only thing keeping me from losing control. I refused to go on sleeping pills, though. That was a line I wouldn't cross.

Two years had passed since I'd left my hometown behind. I had settled into a new city, started a full-time job, and was adjusting to a new life. But no matter how much I tried to push forward, something wasn't right. While duloxetine, the new medication helped with certain things, it also made me feel drowsy and emotional. I often found myself teetering on the edge of tears for no apparent reason, my mind tangled in a web of confusion. They say things get worse before they get better, and at that point, I was beginning to believe it. I was spiralling, overwhelmed by everything around me. It was then that I was placed under the care of a mental health team. I wasn't sure what that would mean for me or where it would lead.

Then one day, an unexpected opportunity came along. I was offered a coveted position as a paint sprayer. This was a skilled job, one that many would have given anything for. I jumped at the chance without hesitation. The first time I pulled the trigger on that spray gun, something clicked. It felt right, like I was meant to be there. I knew right then and there, I was good at this. I had a natural talent for it. Over time, I became known for the quality of my work. This wasn't just a small-time operation. It was a huge, global engineering company—over 4,000 employees, with offices in 170 countries—and my work was getting noticed. The parts I sprayed were being used all over the world. That pride in my work kept me going, even on the darkest days. The money was good, too. I was earning more than I had ever thought possible.

As it turned out, things deteriorated. I tried to end it all. I had reached the point where I couldn't bear it anymore and I thought I would just end it all in the top stairwell of the Victorian house I had my rented room in. I was so lost in my own pain, trapped in a cycle of hopelessness that I didn't see any other way out. I honestly don't know what would have happened if it hadn't been for a guy working the night shift. He had just come in, and I am sure even now, he does not know the impact his presence had that day. If he had not found me, I do not know if I would be here now. That moment, which split second, could have changed everything.

Instead, I was under the priory hospital for four weeks, I was under the watchful care of the mental health team, and for the first time, I felt like someone was looking out for me. But even in the safety of the hospital, the weight of it all still crushed me. I was not just there because of my mental state; I was also battling a recurring drinking problem. It felt like everything I had been hiding was finally out in the open, and it hurt. I was not proud of any of it, especially the fact that I had ever considered taking my own life. I was ashamed, so deeply ashamed. I was starting a journey, but it was a journey that terrified me, and I had no idea what was ahead.

What made it even harder was the fact that I was completely alone in this. I had not told anyone about what was really happening. The only person I eventually told was my mum years later, in 2019, when I started my Facebook page. I had kept this secret for so long, buried it deep inside, too ashamed to share it with anyone. It was not just my mum I had kept in the dark, though. My co-workers had no idea. They knew I was struggling; they knew I was in a low mood, but they only saw the surface. All they knew was that I was off work, that I had a sick note, and that I was not in the best of spirits. They did not know the full extent of my pain. The only thing that seemed to help me get through the day was taking more diazepam alongside my duloxetine. I needed it, just to keep going, to numb the emotions that kept creeping up on me.

The only thing that made me feel strong was my ability to do a good day's work. When I walked into that workshop and picked up a spray gun, I felt at home. It was the one place where I did not have to pretend. The paint was my canvas, the spray gun my brush. Everything else faded into the background when I was working. It was the one thing I could control, the one thing on which I could rely.

Now, four years had passed since I had moved to Bath. I had managed to get a grip on my alcohol consumption, keeping it in check for the sake of my mental health. Work had kept me busy, and I had been in and out of a few relationships. None of them worked out, though. There was one I deeply regretted, where I had cheated on a girl. I do not know what I was thinking. The guilt was unbearable, and even now, it lingers. I cannot change what happened, but I have learned from it. Nobody is perfect. The lesson was hard, but it was one I needed to learn.

By now, I had been living in a house share for four years. I had a stable, well-paid job, and I felt like my mental health was starting to balance out again for the first time in years. I was on 160mg of Duloxatine, seeing my counsellor regularly, and people were leaving me alone. It was a quiet peace I was not used to, but I appreciated it. It felt like a small victory, a moment of calm in a life that had been anything but peaceful.

Then, I found a flat in Bristol. It was not too far from Bath, so I could still drive to work every day. The flat was nice, in a good area, and it seemed like a new adventure. The surroundings were different, and I felt like it was time for another change. I still kept to myself, like I always had. But moving into the flat felt like another fresh start. Maybe this time, I would get it right.

Before I knew it, seven years had passed since I had left my hometown—the one I'd always wanted to escape. I'd just turned 38, and I felt like the past was finally behind me. The weight of it had shifted, and for the first time, I felt like I could breathe again. The demons didn't control me the way they used to. Or so I thought.

At work, I thrived. I was good with my hands—painting, spraying, anything to do with my job. Paint spraying wasn't just a skill for me—it was an art. The sound of the spray gun, the feel of it in my hand, the way the paint flowed smoothly onto the surface, it all felt like something I was born to do. Knowing that my work was going to be shipped globally gave me a sense of pride that nothing else could. It was a part of me, and it felt good to be good at something again.

But the pressure was mounting. Management started pushing me harder, wanting more from me. The hours were stretching out to be a lot longer. Seven days a week, sometimes. The equipment was breaking down, the spray guns were worn out, and the paint pumps were on their last legs. But still, I was expected to deliver. I was working with old, unreliable tools, trying to make them work. They wouldn't give me anything new, and I was expected to perform like a machine. The demands kept increasing, and my health—mentally and physically—was starting to crack under the strain.

The pressure was unbearable. And to make matters worse, my manager—a bully—made everything unbearable. He pushed me harder, berating me when things went wrong, even when things were out of my control. I started losing weight, my face growing gaunt as the stress ate away at me. I was exhausted, both mentally and physically. My behaviour was changing, and I started becoming someone I didn't recognise—ashamed, weak. It made me question everything. Was I doing something wrong? Was I not good enough?

But the more I gave, the more they demanded. It felt like I was trapped in a never-ending loop. An exhausting hamster wheel. I kept delivering decent work, but it was never enough. They always wanted more.

Then, one day, enough was enough. The frustration had been building for months, and I couldn't hold it in anymore. I snapped. I told the manager exactly where to go and spat on the floor in front of him. I had no respect left for him, and I wasn't going to take it anymore.

His face went bright red with rage. But that was nothing compared to what I had endured. "I'm going to HR," I told him. It wasn't a threat—it was my only option. I had to stand up for myself.

Later, he called me into his office, trying to bribe me with more money and extra help. But I had already made up my mind. I couldn't stay in that toxic environment anymore. I had already found a new job—a delivery job. It was a huge pay cut, £17,000 less, but I needed out. The toxic atmosphere was suffocating, and I was done. No amount of money was worth my sanity.

And so, I walked away. It wasn't easy. But I had to take control of my life, for the first time in a long while. The future was uncertain, but for once, I felt like I was making the right choice. And that was enough.

Chapter Seven
A Fresh Start

While I was on my first-ever long weekend in Blackpool, enjoying a much-needed break from the pressures of work, I got a call that would change the course of my life. The voice on the other end was calm and professional, but I could hear the excitement underneath. "Hello, is that Bryan?" the voice asked. "Hello, I am calling you because we specialise in the repair of spray paint pumps and guns. We've seen your work and were wondering if you'd be interested in a trainee position. You'd be shadowing one of our top engineers."

For a moment, I couldn't process what I was hearing. Me? A trainee technician? I had a lifetime of experience with spray paint equipment, but I'd never thought of myself as a technician, never considered the idea that someone might think I could learn to fix them. It felt surreal, but also like a door opening—a door I had long dreamed of walking through.

"Absolutely!" I said before I could stop myself. "I'd love that opportunity."

That call, that one unexpected moment, changed everything. It was more than just a job offer; it was the first step towards a future I had never dared to envision. Now, as I turned 40, I felt a shift within me. Age wasn't just a number—it felt like a turning point. I finally had control over my life, like I was stepping into something real. There was a sense of clarity that had eluded me for years. The chaos in my mind had begun to settle.

The job was not just any service engineer's position. This was a special role, one of only eight in the entire country. A position like that carried immense responsibility, but it also opened doors to opportunities I had never dreamed would be available to me. I could travel, work abroad, and gain expertise in a field so rare, it made me feel like I was on the cusp of something truly extraordinary. The thought of it filled me with excitement, yes, but also dread—dread because the path ahead felt as daunting as it was thrilling.

This was more than just fixing pumps and spray guns. It was an art—just as I had always enjoyed using my hands to create, now I would be using them to fix things, to make them work again. There was something deeply satisfying about the process of restoring something complex and broken. Each component I fixed, each system I repaired, felt like an achievement. The deeper I delved into the work, the more I realised that this was my future. This was what I was meant to do.

The pay? Well, that was another huge bonus. Starting as a trainee, I would earn a substantial salary. But once I became fully competent, the potential pay packet would be life changing. The kind of money I had never even dared to imagine. It was laid out in front of me, ready to be grasped.

But this job wasn't about the money alone. It was about respect. It was about being valued for the first time in years. I had always felt like an outsider, like a broken cog in a well-oiled machine. But now, I had a role that mattered. I had something to prove, not just to others, but to myself. I wasn't just going through the motions anymore; I was building something real, something that had purpose.

At the same time, something else was changing in my life. I had met someone. A girl. Her name was Deb, and she came into my life like a breath of fresh air. From the moment we started talking, we clicked. It was as if we'd known each other for years. I couldn't remember the last time I had felt so at ease with someone. Conversations with her felt natural, easy. We could talk for hours about anything, and her calm warmth always made me feel safe. Something I hadn't felt before in a relationship.

Right from the start, I was upfront with her. "Deb, you need to know this," I told her one evening, the weight of my confession heavy in my chest. "I have mental health problems." I wasn't going to hide it from her. It had been my shadow for so long, and I wasn't about to start pretending that everything was perfect.

Her response took me by surprise. She didn't flinch. She didn't look at me with pity. She simply said, "I love you for you." Her voice was so calm, so sincere, it nearly broke me. *I love you for you.* Those words, simple as they were, hit me harder than I could have ever imagined. She accepted all of me—the good, the bad, the parts I had spent so long hiding. And for the first time in years, I felt like I didn't have to hide anymore. I could be myself. I could be whole.

Months went by, and things just felt right. Everything was easy, comfortable, like we had been meant to be together. We moved in together, and the sense of stability I had craved for so long settled over me. Deb was my anchor. I felt like I was enough—not broken, not damaged—just me. The fear of letting anyone in, the walls I had built so high over the years, started to come down. With her, I felt safe.

I started thinking about the future. We could get married. We could have kids. I began to dream again, something I hadn't done in so long. I hadn't dared to dream about a life with someone. But now, it didn't seem so impossible. It felt real.

I was still on my journey with mental health, but now I wasn't alone. I moved in with Deb, but I kept seeing the same doctors. They understood me, they knew my history, and that was important to me. It wasn't just about Deb. I had moved because I valued the support I received from my doctor. I needed someone who listened, who didn't just tell me to "pull yourself together." No, they understood that mental health wasn't something you could just "get over." They recognised that it was a journey, and they were there to help me through it.

But my new chapter wasn't without its challenges. I was on the move again—this time figuratively, not just physically. I was growing, changing, and with change came pressure. The job change was huge. The relationship was huge. With both came an immense amount of responsibility. The weight of it all was heavy at times. I had to prove myself in a role that wasn't just about performance—it was about learning, too. The transition wasn't smooth, and I faltered at times. But it was mine to navigate, and I was determined to succeed.

I still remember the first day I stepped into the service engineer role. My hands were shaking a little, my heart was pounding in my chest. But I was ready. I had never been surer of anything in my life. This was the right path. I could feel it in my bones. And as I stood there, learning new skills and fixing complex equipment, the thought crossed my mind: *This is my future*. Each fix, each repair was another step toward proving to myself that I could do this. I could do it well.

I wasn't just surviving anymore. I was living, thriving. And for the first time, I was proud of what I had achieved. I was proud of the person I was becoming.

So, there I was at 40—on the edge of something new. A career I never thought possible. A relationship I never imagined would exist for me. And for the first time in a long time, I could see the road ahead clearly. I wasn't alone anymore. And there was still so much more to come.

Chapter Eight

Opportunity

I was once again filled with excitement about the endless possibilities ahead. I was ready to take on the world. The time passed quickly. I was getting on with it, enjoying my new job where I took machinery apart, pulling it to pieces before fixing them.

This was by far the most challenging job I had ever had. I could finally get my teeth into something—really assess myself. It was hard, so much to learn, but it kept me engaged. I was hungry to know more, to do more. The days seemed to fly by, and I felt the thrill of progress with every machine I tackled. But then something started to shift.

The guy who had been training me began disappearing increasingly. At first, I didn't mind too much. I could manage things on my own. I needed that independence, that confidence, to know I could fix these machines by myself. But the problem was, there were so many different machines to learn about. Each one had its quirks, its complications. I'd think I had something figured out, only to realise I needed help. I'd ask for it, but there was always some excuse—something that got in the way.

For six days, I tried my best to fix five different machines. I got stuck each time, left to struggle on my own. Eventually, I gave up on some and started working on others. It was too much, the pressure was mounting, and it wasn't just affecting me. It was affecting my girlfriend—now my fiancée. She could see it, could feel it. I didn't want to drag her into my mess, but I could see the worry in her eyes.

I thought this would be my time—the time for me to finally get things right, to live the life I'd always wanted. I thought it was my chance to be liked, to finally prove myself. But that dream began to shatter. I could feel it. The bullying I had suffered for years seemed to be creeping back in.

I had to confront the trainer. But every step I took toward that confrontation felt like walking on broken glass. It was like he wasn't the same person anymore. When I finally spoke up, when I asked for help, his response was cold. It was as if he didn't even care anymore. He'd changed overnight.

I couldn't take it anymore. I walked straight into the manager's office. It was a family-run business, and I hoped, maybe foolishly, that someone would listen to me. I told the manager everything. I told him I wasn't getting the support I needed, that I felt completely abandoned. He just sat there, clueless, like he didn't even hear me. Then the trainer came in, and it was me against both of them. I've been in this position before. It was happening again.

The trainer flat-out denied everything. I was made to look like a liar, as if I was just making it all up. My mind started racing, thoughts flooding in from all parts of my life—the accident when I was 18, the court case I had fought so hard for, and now this, at 41! Why was this still happening to me?

I couldn't hold it in anymore. I stood up, looked at both of them, and said, "You arseholes!" The trainer had the audacity to laugh behind the manager's back. At that moment, I knew I wasn't going to be heard, and feeling helpless, I just walked out.

It felt like a weight had been lifted, but it was also terrifying. For the first time in my life, I had walked out of a job. I had left behind something that could have been my future, a dream job I thought was mine. I felt a rush of emotions—relief, fear, confusion. I stepped outside and called Deb, my fiancée. I told her what I had done. She couldn't believe it at first. To this day, nearly ten years later, she still can't fully grasp it.

So, there I was, jobless. But I knew that it was completely the right thing to do. I had been down the bullying road too many times before. I just couldn't take it anymore, mentally, or physically. Deb understood. She supported me, even though I felt so broken.

The problem was, I was turning to drinking heavily again, slipping back into old habits. The drugs crept back into my life, and I felt like I was sinking. I stopped taking my duloxetine completely missed doses and let everything slip. My mental health was plummeting, and I didn't know where to turn. I needed help. I needed someone to listen. I'd found a new doctor through Deb's surgery, but the weight on me was still heavy.

The next two weeks were a blur. I spent them in bed, barely moving, barely speaking to anyone. I felt worthless, like a shadow of the person I used to be. Cans of lager piled up beside me, and the smell of weed permeated Deb's flat. I had tried so hard to be normal, but I just didn't feel like I was getting a fair shot. Every time I managed to get on my feet and get a step up; I was knocked down again.

When the two weeks had passed, I knew I had to pull myself together. I had to find some strength, because for the first time since I was 16, I was unemployed. It wasn't because of redundancy—it was because I'd been broken too many times by the same bullying, the same mistreatment. I couldn't let it beat me anymore.

I've had some incredibly valuable opportunities taken away from me over the years, all due to the destructive nature of bullying.

Deb and I went to a job agency, and I signed up to look for work. The same day, I met a new doctor, and my medical notes were transferred over. It was August 2nd, 2015, when the new doctor reviewed my medication —duloxetine, 160mg a day. I also had diazepam to help me relax. My antidepressants had been getting stronger and stronger over the years, and it was clear that I needed them now more than ever. This was my 25th year on antidepressants.

Chapter Nine

Family of Three!

I was finally settling into a job I could rely on, working as grounds maintenance for a housing association. It was only seasonal, but it was a wage, and that was something I hadn't had in a while. I actually felt like I had a chance to challenge myself again, like I could take on whatever life threw at me. It was a new sense of hope, something I hadn't felt in years.

The months flew by, and I must have made an impact because in October of 2015, I was asked if I wanted to move into the cleaning department as a mobile cleaner. It wasn't the most glamorous job in the world, but it was stable. More importantly, it grounded me. It was the first time in my life that I had felt valued in a workplace. The management was supportive, and for once, I felt like I was part of something. It was a feeling I had always wanted.

Things were looking up. I was engaged to Deb, and we were set to get married in September 2016. We were moving forward, building a life together, and for the first time in years, I felt like I could breathe. Everything seemed as though, finally, it was falling into place.

But just as I was daring to think that maybe, just maybe, life was finally being kind to me, another challenge hit. It wasn't just something I had to face; it was something Deb and I had to face together, and it hit her much harder than it hit me. Deb had turned 40, but she couldn't have children naturally and we both knew we wanted children.

We went to the doctor, desperate for answers. After some tests and consultations, we were told that Deb had one free shot at IVF. It was a long shot, but we had to take it. Deb started her treatment on April 26th, 2016. The process was tough—she had to inject herself daily, something that was mentally and physically draining. But the worst part was that the treatment didn't seem to be working. Her body wasn't producing enough eggs.

Then, after a few rounds of stronger treatments, something incredible happened. After a test, Deb produced one egg. Just one. That phone call from the hospital, on May 27th, 2016, was the moment everything changed. We were told to come in, and my heart was racing in my chest. But that wasn't all—while Deb went into another room for her procedure, I was taken into a small room myself, handed a copy of Nuts magazine. Nothing special, just a standard thing they did, or so I thought.

I tried to use my phone to find something better, but of course, the signal was terrible. So, there I was, stuck with nothing but my own imagination. It sounds silly now, but at the time, it was the most intense and awkward experience I've ever had. Still, somehow, it worked, and I managed to do what I had to do. Straight into the pot, keeping it cool, as you're meant to.

It was the May bank holiday weekend of 2016, and the next big step was coming: the embryo transfer. It was exciting, nerve-wracking, and overwhelming. The doctors told us, there and then, that we had a 12% chance of success—that was all. A 12% chance that Deb would get pregnant. We both stood there, hearts pounding in our chests, knowing this was our one shot, our only shot.

So, we waited. The next couple of weeks were torture—waiting, wondering, hoping. On June 12th, 2016, we got the news. It was a miracle. Deb was pregnant. It was unbelievable. We couldn't stop smiling, crying, laughing. It felt like the world had opened up to us, and everything had changed.

On June 30th, Deb had her first scan. I'll never forget that moment, seeing the tiny flicker of the heartbeat on the screen. We were beyond excited. There was hope. There was life. It felt like everything we had dreamed of was finally coming true.

Now we had to focus on the next important thing: our wedding. Set for September 6th, 2016, with Deb four months pregnant, it was a whirlwind of planning, stress, and joy. We managed to pull everything together and on a beautiful September day, we got married. It wasn't just a celebration of our love; it was a celebration of everything we had been through, everything we had survived. Things were great. Our future looked brighter than it ever had.

But just when I was starting to believe my bad luck was behind me, in October, I was hit with a shock to the system. Occupational health at work gave me a lung function test, and I remember, even now, how it felt—like I was standing at the edge of something I wasn't ready to face. When I think back on it, I can't help but feel that someone, somewhere, was looking out for me. You'll understand why when you read more in another chapter, but for now, all I knew was that the test came back normal, but there was an obstruction.

At the time, I didn't think much of it. I'd been in the engineering industry for years, welding, building septic tanks with fibreglass, and then I was a paint sprayer for a long time. Let's not forget the 31 years of smoking and smoking weed. It was no surprise that something wasn't right with my lungs. I'd spent most of my life ignoring the consequences, thinking I was invincible. But now, I couldn't escape it.

I went to see a doctor, and what he told me hit me harder than I ever imagined. COPD—chronic obstructive pulmonary disease.

Chronic Obstructive Pulmonary Disease (COPD) is a progressive lung disease that makes it difficult to breathe. It is characterised by long-term damage to the lungs, which results in airflow limitation and difficulty in getting enough air into and out of the lungs. COPD includes conditions such as emphysema and chronic bronchitis, often occurring together.

In COPD, the airways become inflamed and narrowed, leading to symptoms like shortness of breath, a persistent cough, and wheezing. Over time, the damage to the lungs can become more severe, making it harder for individuals to perform everyday tasks. COPD is primarily caused by long-term exposure to harmful substances, with smoking being the most common cause. However, exposure to air pollution, dust, chemicals, and genetic factors can also contribute to the disease.

The symptoms of COPD can worsen over time, and flare-ups or exacerbations can occur, where the symptoms suddenly become more severe, often triggered by infections or environmental factors. While COPD is a chronic condition with no cure, treatment options are available to manage the symptoms, slow the progression of the disease, and improve the quality of life. These treatments can include medications, inhalers, oxygen therapy, and lifestyle changes such as quitting smoking and staying active.

COPD can significantly impact a person's daily life, limiting their ability to engage in physical activities, and, in severe cases, can lead to respiratory failure or other complications. Early diagnosis and intervention are key to managing the disease and improving outcomes.

I was only 41 years old. I couldn't wrap my head around it! I thought only old people got that type of lung disease. But there it was. It was a punch to the gut. The doctor told me that I needed to stop smoking. I wanted to. I knew I had to. But how? At that point, my life felt like a whirlwind—Deb and I were in the middle of planning our wedding, going through IVF, and searching for a house to buy. How could I just stop smoking when it had been such a part of my life for so long? It was like asking me to give up a part of myself. But I knew it would make the COPD worse. The thought of that terrified me.

Fast forward, and there was some good news, something to hold onto through all of this. We were going to have a baby boy. It was the one thing that kept me going. He was due on the 20th of February, the same day as my birthday. I thought, *wow*, what a miracle that would be. A son born on the same day as me—it felt like fate. But as much as I wanted to stop smoking for him, for Deb, I found myself smoking more. It was like I couldn't break free from the habit, no matter how hard I tried.

Deb was incredible throughout everything, though. I still don't know how she did it. She was amazing, always calm, always supportive. What a woman. But even with her strength, I knew I was letting her down. I needed to quit for our family, for the baby, but it just seemed impossible. With every pack I smoked, I vowed it would be my last. But it never was.

Then, on February 21st, the day after my birthday, our miracle boy, Alfie, was born. I couldn't believe it. After all the struggles, all the uncertainty, he was finally here. And Deb, well, of course, she was amazing. Mother and baby were both doing really well, and I couldn't have been prouder.

When I held Alfie for the first time, skin to skin, my heart swelled so much it felt as though it would burst. Instantly, I loved him more than anything. I remember looking at him and feeling this overwhelming sense of love, like nothing else mattered. But there was something I couldn't quite shake. I wanted to change his nappies; to be the dad he needed me to be, but I couldn't. Every time I looked at him, I saw myself as the little boy I had once been. I could see my younger self, and it terrified me.

It wasn't bad feelings, not about Alfie; it was the bad memories about me. It was like I was seeing ghosts, haunted by memories of my childhood, of the times when I'd had accidents, when I didn't feel in control. It was all too much. I couldn't explain it, but I had to tell Deb and my mum. Even to this day, I still can't bring myself to change his nappies. It's like a part of me is stuck in that moment, forever trapped. I call Alfie my "Wolfe," my little fighter, but sometimes, I feel like I'm fighting against myself.

In 2019, we bought a house together. It felt like the start of something new, a fresh chapter. But reality hit hard when I went back to the doctor four years after being diagnosed with COPD. I hadn't stopped smoking and although I tried hard to ignore it, I knew deep down something wasn't right with my breathing. Sometimes, I'd get short of breath for no reason, and it scared me. I couldn't ignore it any longer. I had to face the truth.

I went in for a lung function test. The results when they came back were bad—though not the worst. It was confirmed. The COPD was worse than they had previously thought. My lungs had suffered permanent damage. The news hit me like a ton of bricks. I felt like I was running out of time, that I'd wasted so many years ignoring the signs. Now, the damage was done, and there was no turning back. It was a constant reminder of my mistakes, and I couldn't escape it.

Chapter Ten

The Ultimate Betrayal

He had once again done something I never thought he would. He had made my wife, Deb, look like a liar, denying things that were absolutely true. It wasn't just the lies; it was the way he did it. The way he turned the truth upside down, twisting everything to suit his narrative. I watched as he hurt Deb, and it cut me to the bone. To see him do that to her, after everything we had been through, was something I never expected. I thought maybe, just maybe, he had changed. That he had learned from the past, that he could finally be the father I had always wanted him to be. But no. Lies. Endless lies.

The pain in Deb's eyes when he denied the truth was something I'll never forget. I could see how much it hurt her, and it crushed me inside. I wanted to scream at him, to confront him, but I couldn't. What was the point? I had been holding onto a hope that he could change, but now I saw that hope was just a fantasy. He wasn't capable of change. He never had been.

The final straw came when I realised that no matter what I did, no matter how hard I tried, he would always be the same. The relationship I had fought so hard to salvage was over. Me and him were no more. I felt a deep, visceral sense of hatred towards him. How could someone who was supposed to love me, protect me, do this? Why couldn't he just be honest with me? Why couldn't he ever see me for who I was? Why couldn't he just be a father?

I couldn't bear the weight of it anymore. The anger, the betrayal, the hurt—it was all too much. I started drinking. More than I ever had before. I thought it would numb the pain; make it all go away. But it didn't. It just made everything worse. It made me feel more lost, more alone. I was drowning in emotions, and alcohol became my escape, my only way to cope. But it wasn't enough. Nothing could fix this. Nothing could take away the heartbreak of realising that the one person I had hoped could be there for me had failed me in the worst conceivable way.

I'm doing my absolute best to be a good dad to our Wolfe. Sometimes, I have flashbacks to when I was younger – memories of when I'd be so scared, to the point of losing control and pooing myself and of course, the countless times I was bullied. Those moments still haunt me, and when I look at Wolfe, I can't help but see myself in him, reminding me of everything I've been through, hoping with everything in me, that he never has to suffer anything similar.

But I know our son will learn from me. He'll see the things I do to look after my mental health, and he'll watch me when I fall. He'll understand, how I get back up on my feet again. Through watching me, he will learn what it really means to cope with the hard stuff life throws at you.

I want my Wolfe to continue what I've started, especially when it comes to mental health, even when I'm not here anymore. He'll know the lessons I've tried to teach him – not just about getting by, but about being strong when it feels impossible. I hope he'll take those lessons with him, share them, and help others along the way.

The Hardest Walk

Chapter Eleven
A Health Anxiety Journey

I went to see the doctor on 15th October 2019, bracing myself for the results of my latest lung function test. When the doctor told me the numbers, it felt like the ground had opened up beneath me. My result was 84%, and I couldn't believe it. It should have been 100%, and the fact that it wasn't, hit me like a freight train. I was in the mild stage of COPD. *Mild stage*, he said. But to me, that was the end of the world. The diagnosis felt like a death sentence.

The doctor, however, was gentle and his voice was calm as he spoke.

"I can only advise you to give up smoking, but then you know that Bryan" he said kindly. His words, though true, were delivered with compassion. He wasn't harsh or condescending—he genuinely cared. But all I could hear was the weight of his advice. He didn't just tell me I needed to quit; he told me I had no choice if I wanted to hold onto whatever was left of my lungs. It was the kind of advice you don't want to hear, but you know deep down it is exactly what you need to. That doctor was incredible. He left the surgery three years later, and even now, I remember him fondly, as the one who opened my eyes to what was really happening to my body.

He said, "What are you going to do now?" His question hung in the air, and I felt the gravity of it, pressing down on me. For the first time, I was forced to face the reality of my life choices.

In that moment, I did something I had never done before. I threw my cigarettes in his bin, looked him straight in the eye, and said, "I need to keep healthy. I'm going to go for a walk." It felt like such a small thing, a single step, but it was monumental to me. I was the kind of person who would get in my car to drive just down the road for a pint of milk. The idea of walking felt alien. Yet, there I was, making that commitment. *I was going to change.*

The next few weeks were a blur. The diagnosis haunted me. The health anxiety took over, and it felt like every breath was a struggle. I couldn't stop thinking about my lungs—*I had lung disease.* Every time I took a breath, it was a reminder of what was wrong, what I had done to myself. I couldn't breathe properly anymore, but I told myself I had to keep walking, even if it was just a little bit each day.

I started walking one mile, then two, then three. Before I knew it, I was walking five miles a day. It became my obsession, my way to deal with everything. But there was more to it. I wasn't just walking to strengthen my lungs—I was walking to keep my mind from falling apart. The more I walked, the less I thought about the fear that gripped me every time I had trouble breathing.

But the anxiety didn't stop. It was like a constant companion, following me everywhere. I started phoning my doctors, three, sometimes four times a week, convinced something was wrong. It wasn't enough to just walk; I needed to know I wasn't alone in this. I needed someone to tell me it was all going to be OK. It was so bad that I ended up calling the British Lung Foundation. At one point, I was calling them every day, sometimes up to 60 times a week. It was a lifeline, a way for me to feel heard, even if they couldn't solve my problems.

But they did help. They assured me that my breathing was more a result of anxiety than the COPD itself. The doctors said the same. But I couldn't accept it. I couldn't stop thinking that my lungs were giving out on me. The doctors gave me advice on how to breathe better, but all I could focus on was the fear. It felt like I couldn't escape it. I was drinking more, googling my symptoms every minute of the day, and making things worse. Yet, at the same time, I was learning. I was educating myself, desperately trying to understand what was happening to me.

Then, on 30th December 2019, I made a decision that would change my life. I created a Facebook page called "The Walking Man from Bristol." It wasn't just for me—it was to connect with other people who were struggling with mental health, to encourage myself and others to get outside and walk. It wasn't about just breathing; it was about finding a purpose, about moving forward. But I made a mistake—I made it a public page, open to the world. And as you'll hear later that decision would come back to haunt me.

By now, Alfie, my son, whom I call my Wolfe, was three years old. He gave me a reason to keep fighting, to push through the fear, the anxiety. He was my motivation, my strength. I had to be there for him, no matter what. Every step I took, every mile I walked, was for him.

I continued to walk, determined to strengthen my lungs and improve my mental health. But the anxiety was a constant battle. I was on diazepam now, in addition to the duloxetine I was already taking. My anxiety was getting worse, but I couldn't stop. I had to keep walking. I was learning to breathe properly again, but the fear still gripped me. I watched YouTube videos of people with severe COPD, convinced that it would soon be me. My breathing felt worse, and I was terrified I was on the brink of something far worse.

But I kept going. I started taking supplements—vitamin D, turmeric, vitamin B, anything that could help. I became addicted to walking. I was walking 20 miles a day at times. It was all-consuming, but it was the only thing that helped. It became my escape.

By 2021, my walking page had started to grow. I was now three years smoke-free, but still, I missed smoking. It was a part of me, something I had done for over three decades. But I had learned to push through. My anxiety was still there, still taking hold of me, but I was getting stronger. I found a mental health charity called Bristol Mind and decided to take on a challenge that would prove to myself just how far I had come.

The challenge was that I would walk 95 miles along the Jurassic Coast, and I would raise money for the charity along the way. It wasn't just a walk—it was a journey, a test of everything I had fought for.

The walk, it turned out, was tough, much harder than I could have ever imagined. On the second day, I hurt my ankle and had to be rescued by the coastguard. A team of twelve had to carry me up a cliff, and the paramedics wanted to take me to a hospital. But I couldn't give up. This walk meant everything to me. It was for the people who had supported me, for the people who understood what I was going through. It was for my mental health, for my son, and for the chance to prove that I was stronger than the fear.

I didn't finish the 95 miles—I managed 78. But in that, I raised £1,300 for Bristol Mind. That walk, with all its pain and hardship, was one of the most important things I've ever done.

Looking back, I can't help but be grateful for the day that occupational health gave me that lung function test. If I hadn't known about my diagnosis, I might have continued destroying my lungs. It scared me, but it also made me realise that I had a choice. I could fight. And I would fight.

In 2020, I stumbled upon a lady on social media whose name was Susie. She was a spiritualist, and at the time, I wasn't really sure what to expect from someone like her.

I looked into it and found out that a **spiritual guide** is someone who helps and supports others on their spiritual journey, offering wisdom, insight, and encouragement. This guide can be a formal figure like a teacher, mentor, or religious leader, or it can be an informal role, taken up by someone with experience and a deep understanding of spiritual matters. Spiritual guides are not necessarily tied to one specific religious tradition—they can come from a variety of backgrounds, including Christianity, Buddhism, Hinduism, or even more eclectic, non-religious spiritual practices. In the UK, as in many other parts of the world, a spiritual guide might offer their services in a range of ways, from one-on-one mentoring and counselling to group workshops or retreats.

The role of a spiritual guide is to help individuals grow spiritually, emotionally, and mentally, assisting them in finding their own path to inner peace, self-awareness, and connection to the divine or the greater universe. While they may offer teachings, they don't impose beliefs or dogma. Instead, their role is to guide, support, and encourage individuals in developing their own unique spiritual practice, often helping them navigate through life's challenges with a deeper sense of meaning.

A spiritual guide helps others to cultivate inner strength, clarity, and self-realisation. They offer guidance on how to live more consciously and authentically, help with personal development, and encourage spiritual practices such as meditation, prayer, mindfulness, and reflection. The guide's purpose is often to provide a safe space for exploration and self-discovery, where the seeker can grow without judgment or pressure. There are certain qualities that spiritual guides normally have in abundance, and Susie had them all:

1. **Wisdom and Knowledge:** A spiritual guide is often someone with a deep understanding of spiritual concepts, whether through their firsthand experiences or formal teachings. This knowledge isn't just academic; it's practical and experiential, drawn from their own life journey. They may have spent years studying spiritual texts, engaged in personal practices, or walked a path of service and self-growth, all of which help them offer insight and perspective to others.

2. **Compassion and Empathy:** A true spiritual guide must have a deep sense of compassion. They understand the struggles that others go through and approach their role with an open heart. They don't simply tell others what to do but listen deeply, offer understanding, and provide the space for their mentee to process their feelings. This empathy helps create a trusting relationship where the seeker feels safe to open up about their spiritual concerns and doubts.

3. **Patience and Non-Judgment:** A key aspect of being a spiritual guide is the ability to be patient and non-judgmental. Spiritual growth can be slow and challenging, and a good guide will respect the pace at which their seeker is moving. They won't push or rush them but instead offer gentle encouragement, knowing that spiritual transformation takes time and that each person's journey is unique.

4. **Authenticity:** A good spiritual guide is authentic, walking the talk. They are not just sharing theoretical knowledge or ideas but living their own spiritual practices and beliefs. They are role models of the spiritual principles they espouse and demonstrate through their own lives the power and peace of their teachings.

5. **Intuition and Insight:** A spiritual guide often relies on their intuition to provide tailored guidance. This can manifest as an ability to sense what is needed in a particular moment or to offer words of wisdom that feel deeply relevant to the seeker's current situation. This intuitive understanding helps them provide advice that resonates on a profound level.

6. **Humility:** A spiritual guide remains humble, knowing that they are facilitators of someone else's journey rather than the ultimate authority. They understand that they are guides, not leaders, and are there to help others discover their own wisdom rather than impose their own ideas. Their humility allows them to be open to learning from those they guide, fostering a reciprocal relationship of growth and understanding.

Spiritual guides use a variety of methods to help you. These methods depend on the guide's own background, training, and philosophy, as well as the needs of the individual. Here are a few common ways that spiritual guides might work:

1. **One-on-One Mentorship:** This is the most personal form of spiritual guidance. In this setting, the guide works directly with the seeker, discussing personal issues, spiritual challenges, and emotional concerns. The relationship between a guide and their mentee is often built on trust, confidentiality, and mutual respect. Through regular sessions, the guide may offer practical advice, meditative practices, or wisdom drawn from their own experience.

2. **Group Workshops and Retreats:** Many spiritual guides offer group sessions or weekend retreats. These can be opportunities for like-minded individuals to come together to learn, reflect, and meditate. The guide might lead group discussions, teach certain practices, and help the group explore spiritual themes in a collective setting. Workshops or retreats can also offer the opportunity to engage in more intense, immersive spiritual practices, such as deep meditation or spiritual rituals.

3. **Spiritual Practices:** A guide will often teach specific spiritual practices that are tailored to the individual's needs. These practices can range from prayer, mantra repetition, and mindfulness to meditation, journaling, and energy work. They might also encourage personal rituals, such as lighting a candle for reflection or creating a sacred space for quiet time. The goal is to help the seeker connect with their inner self and with a higher power or greater universal force.

4. **Providing Spiritual Teachings:** Some spiritual guides take a more formal approach, sharing teachings and spiritual wisdom through books, lectures, or structured lessons. This can be particularly common in religious traditions, such as Christianity, Buddhism, or Hinduism. In these cases, the guide may draw on sacred texts or traditional teachings to help individuals deepen their spiritual understanding and practice.

5. **Counselling and Life Coaching:** Many spiritual guides also offer practical guidance for life's challenges. They may provide advice on relationships, career decisions, health, and personal development, all framed within a spiritual context. This can be particularly helpful for those looking to integrate spiritual wisdom into everyday life and seeking balance between the material and the spiritual.

In the UK, as elsewhere, spiritual guides can be found in many different spiritual and religious traditions. Here are a few examples:

- **In Christianity**, spiritual guides might include priests, monks, nuns, or experienced laypeople who have a deep understanding of Christian teachings. They may guide others through prayer, Bible study, and reflection on the Christian path to holiness.
- **In Buddhism**, spiritual guides are often referred to as "teachers" or "lama." They are knowledgeable in Buddhist practices and philosophy, helping their students through meditation, mindfulness, and the teachings of the Buddha.
- **In Hinduism**, spiritual guides, known as "gurus," are revered for their wisdom and insight. They teach spiritual practices, such as meditation and yoga, and offer guidance on how to live a life in harmony with the divine.
- **In New Age and Eclectic Spirituality**, spiritual guides may not always belong to a specific tradition but instead draw from a variety of spiritual beliefs and practices. They may focus on self-discovery, energy healing, and connection to the universe, helping individuals find their own spiritual path.

Having a spiritual guide can be incredibly beneficial for those on a spiritual journey. A guide offers the experience, wisdom, and support needed to navigate the complexities of personal growth and spiritual awakening. Some of the key benefits of having a spiritual guide include:

- **Clarity and Insight:** A guide can offer a fresh perspective on demanding situations, helping you see things from a higher point of view.
- **Support in Challenging Times:** Life can be full of difficult moments, and having someone to lean on who understands the spiritual aspects of life can be invaluable.
- **Accountability and Encouragement:** A spiritual guide helps keep you focused on your goals and practice, ensuring you stay on track during your journey.
- **Deepening Spiritual Practice:** A guide can help you explore and deepen your spiritual practices, offering advice on how to cultivate mindfulness, prayer, or meditation.

- **Emotional Healing:** Through their wisdom and support, spiritual guides can help with emotional healing, offering a safe space for personal reflection and growth.

A spiritual guide can be an invaluable companion on your journey towards spiritual growth and self-discovery. Whether you're looking for wisdom, support through tough times, or guidance in deepening your practice, a good guide can provide the clarity and insight you need. Their role is to walk alongside you, offering gentle encouragement, teachings, and practices that help you connect with your inner self and the greater universe. It's not about giving you all the answers but helping you find them within yourself. That certainly turned out to be true of Susie.

For the first time I spoke to Susie, I immediately felt a sense of calm. She offered online readings, and I decided to try it. Little did I know, those readings would end up being a source of comfort and guidance during some of the darkest times of my life. Her insights were incredibly accurate, and she seemed to see things that even I hadn't been able to recognise within myself. She had this way of making you feel seen, like she understood you, even when you couldn't fully understand yourself.

She was not just a spiritual guide; she became a part of my journey, offering me words of wisdom, reassurance, and sometimes, just the space to feel heard. She had her own journey as well, which she shared openly, and it made me realise how interconnected our experiences could be. I got to know her better through her social media, where she is known as Susie Gigg, and her presence was nothing short of heavenly. She has this ability to bring peace to those around her, simply through her words and her energy.

For five years, I continued to have readings with Susie, and during that time, she was there through some of my most challenging moments. Every session felt like a lifeline, a thread connecting me to something greater than myself. As the years went by, I felt a deep bond with her, though we had only ever interacted virtually. It was hard to put into words how much her guidance had meant to me, how much of a positive influence she had on my life, especially when I felt so lost.

Then, in March 2025, after all those years of online conversations, I finally met Susie face to face. The emotions I felt were overwhelming, and I'm not sure I can truly explain it to you. There was an undeniable sense of awe, of gratitude and warmth that filled me the moment I saw her in person. It was a moment that felt surreal, like a full-circle moment where everything that had been built over the years suddenly came together. I had no idea it would feel so deeply emotional, but it did. It was more than just meeting someone I had talked to online for years – it was like meeting someone who had walked beside me through some of my darkest days, offering light and support when I needed it most. That meeting, that moment, will always remain etched in my heart.

His FEV1 3.29 (84%); FVC 5.05(102%); FEV1/FVC 65, TLCO 103.6%, KCO 87%. predicted. Lowest sp02 94%. Reversibility was not tested due to dizziness after firs His Nijmegen questionnaire score was 36 . A hyperventilation provocation test den of dizziness and chest tightness post HV. Baseline PetCO2 was 4.7 and PetC02 p hyperventilation recovery time of 0.51mins. An Alpha-1-antirpsin in 2021 was 1.20 He had a PHQ-9 of 23 which indicates severe depression. He had a max GAD-7 severe anxiety.

84% PREDICTED

MY FIRST CHARITY HIKE FOR BRISTOL MIND in 2021

Chapter Twelve

Getting Stronger

By now, I was desperately trying to get stronger and trying to get a grip on this relentless health anxiety that had taken hold of me. Coming to terms with a physical diagnosis like COPD was hard enough, but the mental toll it was taking on me was worse. I kept looking back to the day when occupational health gave me that lung function test, and I realised how close I had been to not even knowing about the damage I was doing to my lungs. If that test hadn't happened, I would have kept on, oblivious to the ticking time bomb inside me. It scared me to think about how much worse it could have been if I hadn't been made aware.

But even with that knowledge, it was hard to stay on track. I felt trapped in a never-ending cycle of fear and frustration. Then came November 2021. I fell into a deep depression. The weight of everything—my health, my past, my future—felt like it was suffocating me. I began drinking heavily, trying to numb the pain. Whisky became my escape. I would drink bottles of it, trying to forget, trying to get away from myself. The one thing I managed to stay away from, though, was smoking. I don't even know how I did it, but somehow, I stayed smoke-free. I still can't believe it to this day, even though I had been without a cigarette.

One night, I was sitting in a pub, completely out of my mind with the booze and depression. That's when I did something I'll never forget. I exposed his name on Facebook for the entire world to see. I wanted revenge. I was drunk, and the hurt inside me was unbearable. I wanted people to know what he had done to me. I wanted them to see the truth. It made me feel a little better at the time, as strange as it sounds. It was like a release, a small act of defiance.

But it wasn't long before the consequences of my actions hit me and hit me hard. One day, I came home from work and found a letter. A solicitor's letter. He was suing me for defamation of character. It was like a slap in the face. I couldn't believe it. He was going to take me to court over what I had said, even though it was all true. The letter said I had two weeks to respond, and I was in a panic. I needed to find a solicitor, but I didn't even know where to start. My mind was a whirlwind of emotions. This was the last thing I needed. The last thing anyone should have to face is when they're already drowning in mental health issues.

I went to six solicitors before I found one who would take me on. And when I sat down with him, his first words were, "You've got yourself into some troubles here, haven't you?" He looked at me, concerned, as if he could already see the toll this was taking on my mental state. "This is a very serious allegation." He wanted to sue me for speaking the truth. All I had was my mum's testimony, the fact that she had seen him quickly pull back a table fork that was inches from my eye, just before he would have hurt me. I had nothing else. But my solicitor believed me, and slowly, things started to turn around. "You've got a strong case here," he said. "But this will cost thousands in court, and it will be emotionally draining."

Letters flew back and forth between solicitors, the tension building with each passing day. In the end, he got nothing out of me. The case was kicked out of court. But there was a catch. I had to sign a document saying I would never use his name again on social media or anywhere else. I agreed to it, not because I wanted to, but because I knew I had to protect my wife and son. I couldn't risk anything happening to them because of my actions.

Despite that, I still didn't regret what I had done. I had spoken the truth. I wasn't a liar. I stood tall, even though it felt like the ground was crumbling beneath me. But that was the final straw. I hit the whisky again as well as anything else I could get my hands on. I wasn't taking my antidepressants. I was spiralling. I went on a rampage, posting videos on Facebook, expressing my anger, my hurt, my confusion. I was in a terrible state. I didn't want to be here anymore.

One cold Saturday morning, I told Deb that I was going for a walk. I was in such a low place lower than I had been in years. I had never felt so hopeless. I went to the shops, bought a bottle of whisky and some cans of beer, and headed deep into a forest. I spent the entire day there, just drinking, getting more upset and angrier. I hated him. *I hated him so much.* I kept posting videos on my Facebook page, showing just how broken I felt, how lost I was.

At some point, I collapsed in the mud, face down. I remember seeing a light flashing in front of me, and I thought. *This is it*. I thought I saw my hero, my grandad, the person who had always been my guide in life, telling me to get up. But it wasn't him. It was the police. They had found me and the next thing I knew, I was being taken to a hospital. I had hyperthermia. I was lucky to be alive, I was told. My wife had told the police the places I often walked with the dog, and they had found me there.

The following day, I spoke to Deb, and I told her that I had seen my hero. I was convinced it had been him, but it wasn't. It had been the police pulling me back from the edge. This was a new trauma, a fresh wound, brought on by the fact that he wanted to sue me.

I had to take time off from work after that, but my depression only deepened. Days, weeks, and months passed. I was drinking heavily again, not taking care of myself. In November 2022, I had a relapse. I started going into town, drinking whisky, looking for fights. I posted more disturbing videos online, expressing my pain and distress. I wanted someone to hurt me. I didn't care anymore. I thought about suicide constantly - I was planning it in my mind. But two things stopped me—my son and my hero. They kept me holding on, trying to stay here for them.

Then one Friday night, I was found by the police in the middle of the road. Passers-by thought I was dead or had been run over. The ambulance came, but I escaped from it before they could take me to the hospital. I thought they were trying to hurt me. I was terrified. The police chased me through the carport, and when they caught me, they said,

"It's OK, it's OK. You're safe now."

But I was too far gone to understand. I was crying, confused. I thought they were going to kill me.

I was hearing a lot of voices in my head. None of what they said made any sense, but all of them reeked of hatred towards me.

I remember, all the time, Deb was getting text messages from her family, telling her to leave me They said I was fake, that I didn't deserve her. But through it all, Deb was the only one who stood by me. She never gave up on me, even when the world seemed to be falling apart around us.

I was detained under the Mental Health Act for the second time.

The **Mental Health Act** in the UK is a piece of legislation that governs how individuals with mental health disorders are treated and cared for, particularly when they are unable to make decisions about their own care due to their mental health condition. It sets out the powers and procedures that can be used by medical professionals, social services, and the police to provide treatment or care to someone who is mentally ill, especially in situations where they may be a danger to themselves or others. The Act is designed to balance the need for protection with the rights of the individual.

The main aim of the Mental Health Act is to ensure that people with mental health conditions who require care and treatment receive it in a way that protects both their health and their rights. The Act allows for the detention of individuals in a hospital or other secure settings for their own safety, or to prevent harm to others, when they are diagnosed with certain mental health disorders. At the same time, the Act strives to protect the autonomy of individuals as much as possible, ensuring that their rights are respected throughout the process.

However, while it serves an important function in safeguarding both individuals and society, it is also a source of ongoing debate, especially regarding the balance between patient rights and public safety. It continues to evolve, with efforts to make the system fairer and more responsive to the needs of all individuals involved.

The doctors assessed me again and asked what medication I was on. They were concerned. Deb spoke to the doctor, and apparently, they admitted that I had been overlooked. My mental state shouldn't have spiralled so badly the second time. Deb described me as being like someone from *The Shining*, completely out of control, I wasn't even myself anymore.

I remember the mental health doctor, at that time, looking at me with a clinical detachment I could hardly stand. I felt so exposed, so vulnerable, sitting there in that sterile room, waiting for answers. After a long pause, he finally spoke, his words cold and final, like they had been delivered many times before. He said that the symptoms I was experiencing were probably linked to either bipolar disorder or schizophrenia. The way he said it, so matter-of-factly, made everything feel even more real, and at the same time, unreal. It was like hearing the diagnosis of a stranger rather than something that was connected to my own life.

His words hit me hard, though I didn't fully understand what that would mean for me. There was a part of me that had feared hearing something like this for so long, yet another part was almost relieved to finally have a name for the chaos in my mind. I had always felt like something wasn't right, like I was constantly battling invisible forces inside of me, but to hear it put into such clinical terms felt like an earthquake, shaking the ground beneath my feet. It made me question everything I had ever known about myself and the way I saw the world.

Bipolar? Schizophrenia? The labels felt so foreign, so distant from the person I thought I was. Could I really be that? Could I be someone so broken that my mind would betray me like this? I felt a sense of shame creeping in, as if the very essence of who I was had somehow been called into question. The doctor's words seemed to hang in the air, suspended and heavy. I had hoped for something more than this, some kind of reassurance, a light at the end of a tunnel that felt never-ending. Instead, I was left to face the reality of those words alone, knowing that things were about to change in ways I couldn't yet comprehend.

The confusion, the fear, and the sense of isolation all swirled together as I left the doctor's office. I wasn't sure whether to cry, scream, or just sit in silence. All I knew was that this diagnosis had thrown me into an even deeper uncertainty about who I was and what my future would look like. It felt like a life sentence, something I hadn't even had the chance to prepare for.

Eventually, the mental health team diagnosed me with severe depressive psychosis, triggered by years of trauma and no doubt, the alcohol. The psychiatrist put me on new medication, alongside my Duloxetine antidepressants. I was now taking antipsychotic meds—Quetiapine—and diazepam when needed. I was taking more pills than I ever had before, and I felt physically sick. I had put on weight. I needed to help myself. I knew nobody was going to fix me except me.

But then, I found a new charity—Rethink Mental Illness—and it gave me a sense of purpose again. Maybe this time, I could help myself and others. Maybe this time, I could fight.

Rethink Mental Illness is a prominent charity organisation in the UK dedicated to improving the lives of individuals affected by mental illness. Founded in 1972, Rethink Mental Illness operates with a mission to challenge attitudes and change lives, working towards a society where mental health is understood, respected, and supported effectively.

The charity offers a comprehensive range of services aimed at providing practical support, information, and advocacy for people affected by mental health issues. This includes:

1. **Support Services**: Rethink Mental Illness provides direct support through helplines, online communities, and local support groups. These services offer a lifeline to individuals experiencing mental health challenges, ensuring they have access to peer support, guidance, and practical assistance.

2. **Campaigning and Advocacy**: The organization advocates for policy changes and campaigns to raise awareness about mental health issues. By influencing government policies and public perceptions, Rethink Mental Illness aims to reduce stigma and improve mental health services and support systems.

3. **Information and Resources**: Rethink Mental Illness produces a wealth of information resources, including guides, factsheets, and online content. These resources are designed to educate and empower individuals affected by mental illness, as well as their families and caregivers, equipping them with knowledge to navigate the complexities of mental health.

4. **Training and Workshops**: The charity offers training sessions and workshops for healthcare professionals, employers, and the general public. These initiatives aim to increase the understanding of mental health issues, promote early intervention, and foster supportive environments in workplaces and communities.

5. **Research and Innovation**: Rethink Mental Illness supports research initiatives aimed at advancing understanding of mental health conditions and improving treatment options. By funding research and collaborating with academic institutions, the charity contributes to the development of evidence-based practices and interventions.

6. **Crisis Support**: In times of crisis, Rethink Mental Illness provides immediate support through crisis intervention teams and emergency services. This ensures that individuals in acute distress receive timely and appropriate care, reducing the risk of harm and promoting recovery.

Overall, Rethink Mental Illness plays a crucial role in the mental health landscape of the UK by advocating for change, providing essential support services, and empowering individuals and communities to address mental health challenges effectively. Their holistic approach aims to create a society where everyone affected by mental illness can lead fulfilling lives with dignity and support.

For me, dignity and support are everything when you're living with mental illness. It's not just about having your symptoms treated; it's about feeling like a person again—someone who's valued, respected, and not defined by what's going on in your mind. For a lot of us, mental illness can make you feel like you've lost a part of yourself, or like you're not good enough, because society often treats mental health differently to physical health. But dignity? Dignity means people see you as a whole person, not just your diagnosis. It's about being recognised for who you are, not just what you're struggling with.

When you're living with something like depression, anxiety, or any mental health condition, it's easy to feel isolated, misunderstood, or ashamed. There's so much stigma out there, and you can end up feeling like you're the problem, like it's your fault. But when people treat you with dignity, it makes all the difference. It's like being reminded that you matter, no matter what's happening inside your head. That's what gives you the strength to keep going, to keep fighting for yourself.

Then comes support. Honestly, when you're in the middle of a mental health crisis, just having someone there to talk to can change everything. It's not just about getting advice, though that helps—it's about knowing you're not alone. It's about having someone who listens without judgement, who's there with the right kind of care. It's easy to shut yourself off from the world, but when you have support, you start to see that it's okay to need others, that you don't have to do this on your own. Support helps you feel safe enough to open up, to find your feet again, and to rebuild. Without that, the darkness feels even darker.

But the thing is, dignity and support go hand in hand. One doesn't really work without the other. If you don't feel like you're being treated with respect, it's hard to accept help, and if you don't have help, it's hard to hold on to your dignity. They both need to be there to get through the tough times and start healing.

In the end, dignity and support are what make the difference between just surviving and actually living. They remind you that you're still you, and that even when things are tough, you deserve kindness, respect, and care. Without those things, it's all too easy to feel lost. So, yes, dignity and support are everything. They're the basics. They're the foundation that helps you keep going. Rethink Mental Health gives you that.

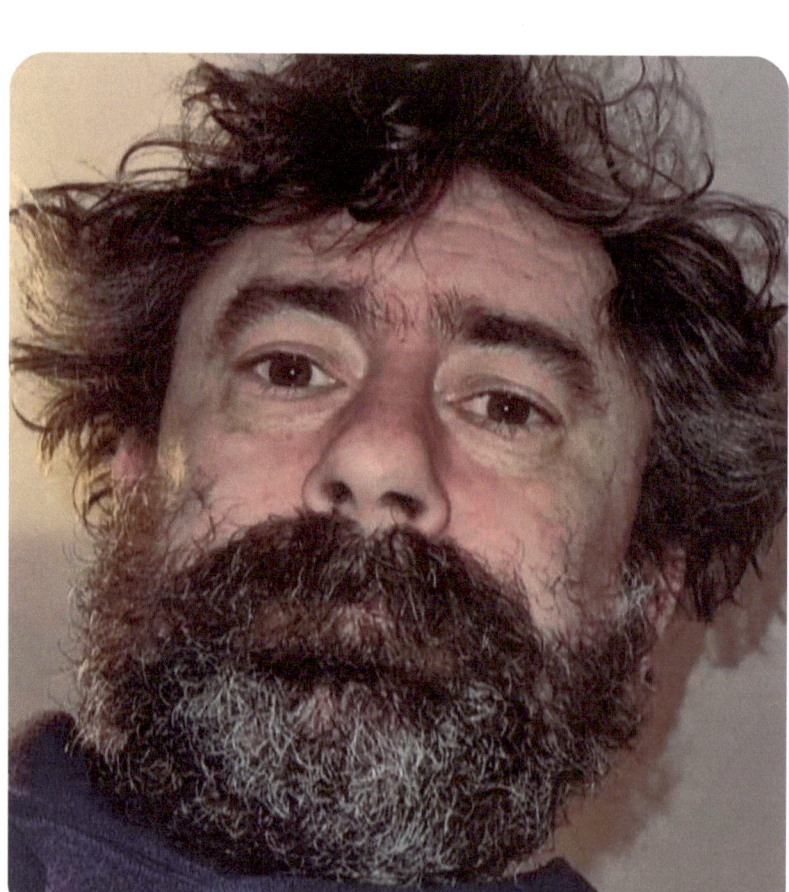

Our Client: Bryan Richard Smith

We have been consulted by Mr Bryan Smith with reference to the pre-action protocol letter of claim which you addressed to him dated the 10th January 2022. We have been instructed to respond to your letter.

We have been through your letter with Mr Smith very carefully and have obtained his instructions generally.

Our client insists that the context of his Facebook Post is substantially correct. We have also discussed the contents of the post with our client's mother who also confirms that so far as the post relates to her it is correct. In the circumstances our client is not prepared to meet your demands as set out on page 5 of your letter.

To try to resolve the matter amicably our client would be prepared to undertake not to repeat his account of events either on Facebook or elsewhere. Other than that he is not prepared to meet your demands.

Your client may care to consider the wisdom of his threatened action. Our client has no money whatsoever. He has borrowed some money to meet our costs responding to your letter. He would certainly not be in a position to pay your client compensation nor costs even in the event of your client's claim succeeding. However rest assured that any claim would be defended. We would respectfully submit that embarking on litigation of this kind would be unwise.

Yours faithfully,

Chapter Thirteen

Making things better

By now, the cocktail of medication I was on seemed to be improving my mental state, antidepressants, and antipsychotic medication. It wasn't an overnight change—it took time, but slowly I started to feel like I was coming back to life. The medication wasn't perfect, but it was helping. My mind was clearer, and I was beginning to feel more like myself, although I still had my moments. But with the improvement in my mental health, my physical health decided to stick the boot in. I was hit with another diagnosis: liver disease. Fatty liver, they called it. On top of that, I found out I had a hiatus hernia that needed to be repaired. My body had definitely been put through the wringer over the years, particularly with alcohol consumption, and it was all finally catching up with me.

In January 2023, I made a decision. It wasn't easy, but I knew it was the right time. I joined Slimming World, with a goal to lose three and a half stone. I was determined. The combination of the medications, my new commitment to my health, and the support I was getting from my Facebook group— "The Walking Man from Bristol"—was propelling me forward. I couldn't believe how much I was starting to achieve. I felt like I was on top of the world. For the first time in years, I felt unstoppable.

When I was high, I was on a complete high, like nothing could touch me, I felt like I could achieve anything I desired. But when I was low, it was a different story and although I still had those low moments, they were fewer and further between. I had more highs than lows, and that made all the difference. I was getting so much support from my Facebook page, more than I ever realised. People were reaching out, telling me that I was helping them with their journey. That was something I hadn't expected.

When I went to my first Slimming World group in January 2023, I was ready to smash it. My first week was a success—I lost 4 lbs. That was just the beginning. I was also scheduled for an appointment with my doctor regarding my hiatus hernia. It was something that needed to be repaired because I had dangerous levels of acid reflux, which wasn't helping with the medication I was on. I believed that if I could lose weight, it would help with my health issues. It would be the push I needed. So, I was referred to a surgeon, and he offered to operate.

It was the beginning of 2023, and things were looking up. I felt more balanced, more grounded. My mental well-being was in a good place, and I had a new sense of purpose. As a week turned into a month, my Facebook group continued to grow. More and more people, from all over, started joining in and supporting each other. It was incredible. It felt like I had found my place in the world.

But then, I set myself a new challenge. I decided to do my second charity walk. This time, it was for Rethink Mental Illness. I had already walked quite a few miles, but this time, I was going to walk 200 miles along the Southwest Coastal Path in June 2023.

In case you are wondering, the Southwest Coast Path is one of the most famous and beautiful walking routes in the UK, stretching about 630 miles (1,014 km) along the coast of Southwest England.

The path kicks off in Minehead, a lovely seaside town in Somerset, right on the edge of Exmoor National Park and takes you all the way to Poole Harbour in Dorset, passing through Devon and Cornwall along the way. This is the northern start of the trail, and right from the beginning, you're hit with breathtaking views of rolling hills and cliffs. The first stretch takes you through Exmoor, where the terrain can be pretty steep and challenging, but the views are absolutely worth it. The path hugs the cliffs, and you'll find yourself surrounded by dramatic landscapes and the sounds of the sea crashing below. Whether you're a seasoned hiker or just someone who enjoys a good walk, this trail has something for everyone – amazing views, pretty villages, sandy beaches, and even a bit of history to take in.

As you continue west, you'll walk through places like Porlock and head towards North Devon, where the cliffs start to get even more dramatic. One of the highlights of this section is Lynton, a village perched above a gorge with incredible views of the coastline. You'll also pass through beautiful spots like Woolacombe and Croyde, both of which are known for their sandy beaches and great surfing.

Next, the path moves into South Devon, a region that's famous for its quaint fishing villages, lush countryside, and the gorgeous English Riviera.

The city of Plymouth is a key stop along this stretch, where you can explore the historic Barbican area, filled with cobbled streets, shops, and cafes.

Moving further along, the towns of Torquay, Paignton, and Brixham make up what's known as the English Riviera. This part of the coast has a Mediterranean feel, with palm trees lining the promenades and stunning views of the sea. The walking here is a bit easier compared to the more rugged north, but you're still treated to some lovely beaches and quiet coves. Maidencombe Beach and Anstey's Cove are peaceful spots where you can take a breather and enjoy the surroundings.

Once you hit Cornwall, the trail gets even more stunning. Cornwall is famous for its dramatic cliffs, golden beaches, and small hidden coves, and the Southwest Coast Path gives you plenty of chances to enjoy it all. St Ives is a charming town that you'll pass through, offering beautiful views of the coastline and a chance to explore its narrow streets full of shops and galleries.

The stretch between St Ives and Land's End is particularly spectacular, with towering cliffs and endless views of the Atlantic Ocean. The path gets pretty wild here, with sea breezes and rugged terrain that make for an exciting (if sometimes challenging) walk. You'll also pass by iconic places like the Minack Theatre, which is carved into the cliffs overlooking the sea, and Mousehole, a lovely little fishing village.

And of course, there's Land's End itself – the most westerly point of mainland England. It's a bit of a tourist hotspot, but it's still an impressive place to visit with dramatic views and windswept landscapes. From here, you can look out across the sea and imagine the vastness of the Atlantic stretching out before you.

After Cornwall, the path enters Dorset, a county known for its jaw-dropping natural landmarks. This section includes some of the most famous spots along the trail, like Lulworth Cove and Durdle Door. Lulworth Cove is a stunning bay with clear waters and a unique, crescent-shaped coastline. It's a wonderful place to stop and relax before continuing on the trail.

Just a short walk along the coast is Durdle Door, an iconic limestone arch that stands proudly in the sea. It's one of the most photographed spots on the path, and once you see it, you'll understand why. The cliffs here are white and dramatic, and the turquoise sea below makes for some truly incredible views. It's a bit of a climb to get to the best views, but it's totally worth the effort.

The last stretch of the path takes you towards Poole Harbour in Dorset, which is one of the largest natural harbours in the world. The area is known for its sandy beaches, scenic views, and relaxed atmosphere. You'll pass through Studland Bay, a lovely nature reserve full of wildlife, before finally reaching Poole, with its historic quay and lovely beaches.

The path ends at Poole Harbour, offering a peaceful culmination to an amazing walk. The views across the harbour are serene, and it's a wonderful place to reflect on the journey you've just completed. From here, you can look back and appreciate the vastness of the coastline you've just explored.

The Southwest Coast Path is one of the UK's most beautiful and rewarding walking trails and I could not wait for my chance to walk it. Whether you're tackling the whole route or just doing sections of it, there's no shortage of incredible views and hidden gems along the way. From the wild cliffs of Exmoor to the sandy beaches of Cornwall, and the dramatic landmarks in Dorset, this trail offers a real adventure. It's a chance to get out in nature, enjoy some stunning coastal scenery, and explore the unique towns and villages that line the path. If you're looking for a proper challenge or just a fantastic way to spend time outdoors, the Southwest Coast Path is an unforgettable experience.

By this point, I had been smoke-free for nearly four years, and my lung strength had improved. My confidence and determination were through the roof. I was on fire, and I was determined to make a difference. My journey with Slimming World was going great, too. By June, I had lost over two and a half stone, and I was ready to face the challenge ahead.

But, just three days before my big adventure, I got a phone call from the hospital and disaster struck. They had scheduled my surgery. It was the moment I had been waiting for—much-needed surgery that could change everything. The surgery appointment clashed with my charity walk. I was shattered. I had been training for six months, preparing myself mentally and physically for the 200-mile walk, and now I had to face the possibility of rescheduling. I pleaded with the hospital to move the appointment, explaining how important both things were to me. They gave me no choice except to be put back on the waiting list.

Despite the setback, I went ahead with the walk. And let me tell you, it was no easy feat. My feet were covered in blisters, and I was tired unbelievably, but I kept pushing. I walked 200 miles over 15 days, blogging and sharing videos on my Facebook page, "The Walking Man from Bristol." I was carrying a charity shaker and raising money for Rethink Mental Illness. By the end of it all, I had raised £1,200. It felt like the most incredible achievement. I had made it.

My first way in tonight I've lost 4 LBS I buckled today and i have had a serge for bad foods but I will take that 4lbs

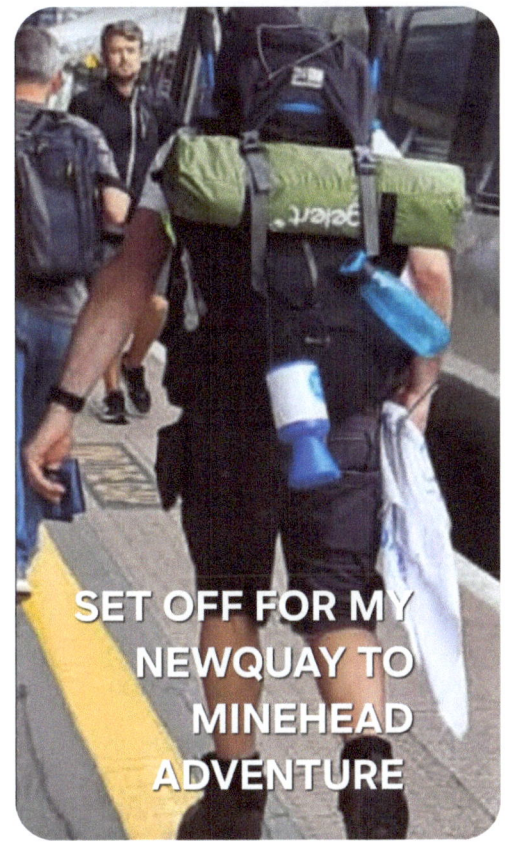

Bryan Smith

Chapter Fourteen

My Story Isn't Over

But my journey didn't end there. I felt this buzz, this excitement about charity work, and before I knew it, I had decided to take on more charity events. I planned another hike for 2024. These events were all in support of Rethink Mental Illness, and I was determined to make a real difference.

Two weeks after my 200-mile adventure, I was back at the hospital for my next surgery appointment. This one was scheduled for August. I was relieved that it was finally happening, and with my weight loss, I was really feeling more hopeful about the future.

Then, to my huge surprise, I found out that I had won the Man of the Year award from Slimming World. What an incredible shock that was! It was a recognition I never expected, and it filled me with pride. Through Slimming World, I had made some lifelong friends. It felt like all the demanding work, the ups and downs, were finally paying off.

The surgery I had in August went well. It was all about healing now, and I had to focus on watching what I ate. I had come so far, and I wasn't about to let anything derail my progress. My drinking had virtually stopped. Alcohol was no longer a part of my life.

And then, unexpectedly, I got a phone call from Bristol Community Services, part of Rethink Mental Illness. I had won the prestigious "Supporter of the Year" award. They were inviting me to go to London to receive the award, and my travel expenses were covered. I couldn't believe it.

It was November 2023, and here I was, being recognised for all the arduous work I had put in. I was overwhelmed.

Standing in front of a huge crowd in London, I made my speech. I spoke about my journey, my plans for the future, and how I wanted to keep pushing forward. I spoke about my book, *The Hardest Walk*, and my ambition to do a Tandem Jump and walk the coast-to-coast in 2024. I felt incredibly ambitious. The world was at my feet.

But, as always, life had its challenges. My wife, Deb, and I were struggling. Our son, my "Wolfe," was having a tough time. Deb had been through so much with me over the years, and now she was on the verge of a breakdown. I could see it, and it was breaking my heart.

I made the toughest decision of my life. For the sake of Deb and our Wolfe, I decided to leave our family home. It was the hardest thing I've ever done. I was crushed, but deep down, I knew it was the right thing for everyone.

Once again, the hate messages started flooding in. People were saying all sorts of things about me—accusations of affairs and lies. It seemed like nothing would ever change.

But despite everything, Deb and I had supported each other through it all. We had been through the worst, and while this was a tough time, I knew that it was all for the best. Our Wolfe was the one thing that kept us going. We both wanted what was best for him, and sometimes, that meant making the hardest decisions of all.

After a lot of heartache and soul-searching, Deb and I had decided it was time to separate. The decision didn't come easily, but we knew it was for the best. Our separation was amicable—no bitterness, just two people who had tried everything but couldn't make it work anymore. We sold our home, a place full of memories, and in May, I moved to another town, trying to rebuild my life from the ground up.

As upsetting as it all was, we kept a positive outlook, for our son, Wolfe, above all. By now, he was dealing with his own mental health struggles and what scares me and Deb is the fact he is just like me and when he was just four, he'd seen me at my lowest points. Witnessing the darkest days of my life, the trauma of seeing me suffer had left a mark on him. On top of that, the issues he was facing at school heaped more weight on his shoulders. It broke my heart to see him struggle. As he gets older, I'm worried he will end up the way I am Psychiatrists do say that mental health can be genetic, he will not have the childhood I had but me and his mum can only try our best to support him with our own doctor "DR C". Our Wolfie goes on park runs every Saturday with my doctor, so I know he is well cared for.

In June 2024 despite being terrified of heights, I did something I had never thought I would have the courage to do. I took a tandem skydive for charity—Rethink Mental Illness. The thought of jumping out of a plane at

13,000 feet terrified me, but I did it. I raised £1,000 for the charity. The fear was overwhelming, but as I stood there, getting ready to leap out into thin air, I remembered my hero, my grandad, who had always been by my side, even when I didn't realise it. Strapped to me, in the pocket of my jumpsuit, was a small picture of him, that tall figure I had seen when I was young, speaking to my mum. He was with me, just as he had been on every one of my adventures. I knew he would never leave me.

By the time I completed the jump, I had just hit five years smoke-free. To think where I had come from, from that dark place to where I was now. It felt like a miracle. I went to see a top doctor privately, and the change in my COPD was unbelievable. When I was first diagnosed, I had blown into the device and scored 84% on the test, which was already a warning sign. But now, after years of keeping active, eating well, and sticking to my treatment, I blew 96% at that doctor's office. He looked at me and said, "You really should be proud of yourself." And for the first time, I was. I felt like I could breathe again, not just physically, but emotionally too.

My mental health was more balanced than ever, thanks to the right combination of medication. At times, I felt like I had superpowers. The lows were still there, but the highs were so much more frequent now. I could see a future for myself, a future where I wasn't just surviving, but thriving. I began making even bigger plans. I was going to trek through Iceland in March 2026 to raise money, and as I write this, I'm working on my book, *The Hardest Walk*. I want this book to reach as many fellow sufferers as possible, and I've decided that half of the profits will go to Rethink Mental Illness. This is more than just a personal journey; it's about helping others who are going through the same struggles I have faced.

My story, however, isn't over. It's just the beginning. The real challenge still lies ahead: my coast-to-coast walk across the UK. This would be the ultimate test of my strength and determination—192 miles, covering three national parks. I was going to walk through the Lake District, then into the Yorkshire Dales, and finally, through the Yorkshire Moors. This was something I'd never dreamed I'd be capable of, but I knew I had to do it.

The **Coast-to-Coast Walk** is one of the UK's most popular long-distance hikes, and for good reason. It takes you on an unforgettable journey from the Irish Sea in the west all the way to the North Sea in the east, crossing some of the country's most stunning landscapes. Starting in the Lake District and heading through the Yorkshire Dales before finally finishing in the Yorkshire Moors, this walk really does have it all – from rugged peaks to rolling hills and even sweeping coastlines. Being up for an adventure, here's what is I could look forward to along the way.

The walk kicks off at **St. Bee's Head**, a clifftop spot on the Irish Sea. You'll get fantastic views of the coast as you begin your journey, with the sound of waves crashing below. It's a pretty easy start, taking you through farmland and villages as you head into the Lake District. The first section of the walk is fairly flat, but don't worry, things get more exciting soon enough.

The Lake District: Lakes, Fells, and Epic Views

Now we're into the **Lake District**, and this is where the walk gets seriously stunning. It's a mix of gorgeous lakes, steep hills, and towering mountains, with some tougher sections that'll really get your heart pumping.

1. **Ennerdale Water to Borrowdale:** After leaving St. Bee's, you'll follow the path towards Ennerdale Water, a peaceful lake surrounded by woodlands and mountains. From here, the path climbs up into the hills, offering cracking views. This part can be a bit rocky, but it's nothing too bad. Soon you'll be heading down to **Borrowdale**, a beautiful valley full of little villages and riverside walks.

2. **Great Langdale Valley:** As you move further into the Lake District, you'll find yourself in the Great Langdale Valley. The scenery here is next level, with big, dramatic peaks like Scafell Pike – the tallest mountain in England. The path here can get steep and rocky, but you'll be treated to some incredible views of the surrounding landscape as you climb.

3. **Kirk stone Pass and Patterdale:** The next section takes you over Kirkstone Pass, a mountain pass with panoramic views of the valleys below. It's a tough climb, but when you reach the top, the views are totally worth it. After that, you'll head down into Patterdale, a charming village nestled at the foot of Helvellyn, another big peak in the Lakes.

4. **Helvellyn Range:** For those wanting a challenge, the walk crosses the Helvellyn range, one of the most famous parts of the Lake District. This is a tough section, with some scrambling over rocks, but the views are absolutely incredible. You'll see vast lakes, green

valleys, and distant mountains, so if you're up for it, this section will definitely be a highlight.

The Yorkshire Dales: Rolling Hills and Pretty Villages

After leaving the Lake District, the path heads into the **Yorkshire Dales**, where the terrain is a little gentler. The Dales are full of rolling hills, pretty villages, and lush green valleys. The walking here is much easier on the legs, and the scenery is just as stunning.

1. **Keld and Swaledale:** The walk takes you through Keld, a quiet village at the heart of Swaledale. The valley here is lush and green, with stone barns and dry-stone walls marking the landscape. It's a beautiful spot, especially in the spring when the flowers are out. You'll follow quiet country lanes and grassy paths through the dales.

2. **Richmond:** As you head further south, the trail passes through **Richmond**, a lovely market town with a medieval castle. This is a wonderful place to take a break, have a wander around, and maybe grab a bite to eat. From here, you'll walk along the River Swale before heading back into the hills.

3. **The Vale of York:** The path then moves into the Vale of York, where the landscape is more open and flatter. The walking here is pretty relaxed, with lots of farmland and wide, sweeping valleys. It's a peaceful part of the walk that lets you enjoy the quiet beauty of the Dales.

The Yorkshire Moors: Wide Open Spaces and Wild Views

The last part of the walk takes you into the Yorkshire Moors, and this is where it really starts to feel remote and for me, magnificent! The moors are wide, open spaces with miles of heather and grassland. The path across the moors is less challenging in terms of height, but it can still feel tough because it's so vast and exposed. The weather here can change pretty quickly too, so it is best to be prepared for anything!

1. **Cleveland Hills:** Before you fully hit the moors, the path takes you through the Cleveland Hills. It's a nice mix of ridges, valleys, and woodlands, and the views over the surrounding countryside are fantastic. It's a gentler walk than the Lake District but still offers some great panoramas.

2. **North York Moors:** The North York Moors is where the landscape opens up completely. It's all wide, wild spaces, with heather and long grasses stretching out in every direction. It can feel a bit lonely at times, but it's also incredibly peaceful. Along the way, you'll pass through a few small villages, including Rosedale Abbey, a really charming little place with a lovely village green.

3. **The Finish: Robin Hood's Bay:** The final leg of the walk takes you down to **Robin Hood's Bay**, a picturesque fishing village on the coast. This is the moment you've been waiting for – dipping your toes in the North Sea after days of walking through stunning countryside. It's the perfect place to finish the walk, with views across the sea and a well-deserved sense of accomplishment.

I knew that the **Coast-to-Coast Walk** is an epic adventure that would take me through some of the most beautiful parts of England. From the dramatic peaks of the **Lake District** to the rolling hills of the **Yorkshire Dales** and the wild, windswept moors of **Yorkshire**, it's a journey full of variety and stunning views. Whether you're looking for a real physical challenge or just want to explore some incredible landscapes, this walk has something for everyone. So, lace up your boots, pack a bag, and get ready for one of the most rewarding walks of your life.

I set off in September 2024, wild camping for as much of it as I could. I knew it would be a challenge, and I was right, it was one of the hardest things I'd ever done, but also one of the most rewarding. Every step I took, every mile I covered, I was proving to myself that I wasn't defined by my past, by my struggles. I was making something new for myself. I documented the whole thing through video blogs, sharing my journey on my Facebook page.

And I did it. I walked 192 miles, and by the end, I had raised £1,080 for Rethink Mental Illness. It wasn't just about the money. It was about showing others that you can rise above your challenges, no matter how big or small. I felt like I had accomplished something truly meaningful, something that would stay with me forever.

5 YEARS LATER
97% PREDICTED

normal. His blood pressure 148/105 and his oxygen saturation on room air was normal at 98%.

His physical examination was normal. There were no crackles or wheeze, and examination of the cardiovascular system, abdomen and legs revealed no abnormalities.

I note that his detailed lung function tests in April this year have shown only mild obstructive defect with normal gas transfer and normal transfer co-efficient. I also learn that his chest X-ray is normal although may have shown hyperinflation in lung fields.

His spirometry today was pretty much normal despite a slightly reduced FEV1/FVC ratio.

The values are as follows:
- FEV1   3.51   97% predicted
- FVC   5.11   114% predicted
- Peak flow   679   129% predicted
- FEV1/FVC ratio   69%

Chapter Fifteen
It's Just the Beginning

Rethink Mental Health featured me on their website. It was a proud moment and one that made me even more determined to do whatever I could to help others facing mental health issues.

"I've got the support I deserve" – Bryan's story.
14/05/2024

Bryan, <u>our 2023 Supporter of the Year</u>**, writes about his journey living with** anxiety, depression **and** <u>PTSD (post-traumatic stress disorder)</u>.

With support from his family and Rethink services**, Bryan has become The Walking Man from Bristol, walking miles to raise money for severe mental illness.**

I've been struggling with my mental health from the tender age of five years, battling ongoing anxiety since 1989. At the age of 15, I was first put on antidepressants because I was experiencing symptoms of low mood, short temper, nervousness and thoughts of ending my life.

When I was 18, my PTSD (post-traumatic stress disorder) was triggered by a near-fatal traumatic industrial incident, where my right forearm was wrapped around a big industrial pillar drill. I was pulled into the machine, lifted into the air, and swung around like a rag doll. My bones were sticking out of my forearm. I already had some degree of social anxiety creeping in because of being bullied, which led to extremely low mood and depression. It was bad and it only got worse as I grew older.

I had counselling for my PTSD, but that was about it. To this day I still can't watch certain TV programs because it makes me shake and feel like it's happening again, like my right forearm is getting tangled into a machine. Most weeks I have horrific nightmares and sweats, as the dreams feel very real and it makes me cry.

It's gotten better over the years, but you never get over such trauma.

Now in my 40s, I'm on two antidepressants and two antipsychotic pills a day, the latter prescribed to me in 2022. I'm very highly medicated now, my pills getting stronger with higher dosages, but I'm stable. It's possible I'm bipolar or schizophrenic. My family has been told this and now I've been given the definite diagnosis of psychotic depression. I only had two episodes of psychotic depression, but they were the scariest because I was convinced people wanted to kill me, and I was hearing and seeing things.

People need to understand and know the difference between mental health and mental illness. Everyone has mental health, but people can develop mental illness. I try very hard to get this message out there and explain the difference. In this day and age, there is way too much stigma attached to people who have severe mental illnesses.

This is my life now, but it's stable and I'm living my best life. I've got the support that I deserve through Bristol Community Services, Rethink Mental Illness. I have a great relationship with my GP, psychiatrist, slimming group because they have seen me from rock bottom to now. I chose to help myself because I have a little boy, and I want to see him do good and not have the life I've had.

- *Everyone has mental health, but people can develop mental illness.*

I get sick and tired of the stigma that people suffering from mental illness have to put up with. There are so many different degrees of this horrible illness, but what you can do is help yourself and give yourself the best possible quality of life. And that is exactly what I intend to do. I'm a human being that deserves to be here as much as anyone.

Nobody really knows what I've gone and still go through, as no one knows what it's like to walk in my shoes. I intend to spread awareness by being honest and open about my journey, and to make a positive impact on others.

One of the ways I do this is through my Facebook page, called 'The Walking Man from Bristol,' which has gained followers from all over the world. Fundraising for Rethink Mental Illness has also given me a purpose in life to support and help fellow sufferers. I've met so many great people who work for Rethink, who have made me feel safe and a part of the Rethink family.

It has made me immensely proud to see my name linked with this organisation that does so much for so many people. I will certainly continue to do everything I can to support them.

In March 2026, I plan to set out on a charity hike through the wild and rugged landscapes of Iceland, aiming to cover the vast expanse over five challenging days. As I traverse this breathtaking terrain, I hope to witness the awe-inspiring Northern Lights – a spectacle that has captivated my imagination for years. The hike will not only be an adventure but also a deeply personal journey, as all proceeds raised will be dedicated to supporting Rethink Mental Illness, a cause that has been close to my heart for some time.

This challenge is just the beginning. My ambition is to continue organising charity events for the next decade, aiming to raise awareness and funding for mental health, until I reach the age of 60. These events will be a reflection of my commitment to making a difference, to creating a lasting impact in the fight for better mental health support and understanding.

I am driven by the belief that every effort, no matter how small it may seem, has the power to change lives. My role in this is far from over. I will persist in raising awareness, using my voice and actions to continue what I started. Through these endeavours, I hope to inspire others to join me in supporting a cause that affects millions, ensuring that mental health is no longer ignored or misunderstood. This is my mission, and I intend to see it through, with passion and dedication, for as long as I am able.

The moral of my story? People made me who I am today. A lifetime of traumatic events and lies shaped me, but they didn't break me. I spent 35 years on medication to keep me going, and every year, the medication gets stronger, and so do I. But it's not just the medication that's made me stronger—it's the experiences, the lessons, and the people I've met along the way. I will continue raising awareness and doing charity events every year, because there's always more to give.

Here's the thing about bullying:

Bullying: Why It Happens and Its Lasting Impact

Bullying is something that can affect anyone, but it tends to hit hardest with kids and young people who are still figuring out who they are. It can show up in lots of diverse ways—whether it's verbal insults, physical aggression, cyberbullying, or even just excluding someone from a group. Bullying can happen anywhere: schools, workplaces, online spaces, and sometimes even within families. While bullying has always been around, the effect it has on people, and on society, is massive. To really understand it, we need to look at why it happens and the lasting damage it can do to its victims, of which I was certainly one.

Why Does Bullying Happen?

There are a lot of reasons why someone might be a bully. Sometimes it's personal, other times it's more about social or environmental factors. Here are some of the key reasons people might be bullies.

1. **Insecurity and Low Self-Esteem:** A lot of the time, bullying comes from someone's own feelings of insecurity. People who feel bad about themselves might bully others to feel better or more in control. It's a way of putting someone else down to try and lift themselves up. This is especially common in kids and teens, but it can carry on into adulthood too as I discovered to my cost.

2. **Learned Behaviour:** Bullying can sometimes be learned from the way that someone grows up. If a child sees aggression, conflict, or neglect at home, they might think that bullying others is an

acceptable way to deal with their own problems. Peer pressure can also play an important role, especially if someone is trying to fit in with a certain group.

3. **Power Imbalances:** Bullying often happens when there's a power imbalance—like when one person is perceived as weaker or different from the bully. This might be because of their physical size, social status, ethnicity, gender, or any number of things. The bully may feel more powerful by putting down someone who they think is "less than" them. This is something that I can relate to from my childhood experience.

4. **Prejudice and Discrimination:** Unfortunately, some bullying is driven by prejudice. If someone holds biased views about a group of people, whether because of race, religion, sexual orientation, or something else, they might use bullying to express those negative feelings. It can also come from a lack of understanding or empathy for people who are different, which only reinforces harmful stereotypes.

5. **Media Influence:** The media plays a big role in making certain types of behaviour seem normal and that includes bullying. On TV shows, movies, and social media, bullying can sometimes be portrayed as funny or a way to gain power or attention. For young people who are still figuring out social norms, this can send the wrong message, they might get the message that bullying is okay or even cool.

The Short-Term Effects of Bullying

The immediate effects of bullying are often devastating, and they can affect someone in a number of ways, as I experienced when I was a child. These effects aren't always obvious on the outside—some victims of bullying hide their pain very well—but the emotional toll is real.

1. **Emotional and Psychological Strain:** Victims of bullying often experience feelings of anxiety, depression, and hopelessness. The constant fear of being targeted can cause stress, making it hard to concentrate on schoolwork or enjoy social activities. Bullying can make someone feel worthless and as if they don't deserve respect, which can lead to long-term emotional damage.

2. **Social Withdrawal:** Many people who are bullied start to withdraw from others. They might avoid social situations or stop taking part in group activities because they're afraid of being humiliated. This can make things worse, as the victim becomes more isolated and vulnerable to further bullying.

3. **Physical Symptoms:** The emotional strain caused by bullying can show up physically too. Victims might experience headaches, stomach aches, or trouble sleeping and, in my case, soiling myself. In some cases, the stress can lead to more serious issues, like self-harm or even PTSD, especially if the bullying is severe. It's not just a mental problem—it's a physical one as well.

4. **Falling Behind at School:** Bullying can have a massive impact on academic performance. When someone is constantly stressed or worried about bullying, it's really hard to focus on schoolwork. The fear of facing a bully in class can lead to missed school days or poor performance in exams, making it even harder for the victim to succeed academically.

The Long-Term Effects of Bullying

While the short-term effects of bullying are tough enough, the long-term consequences can be even more serious. The emotional scars left by bullying can last for years, and sometimes they don't go away at all.

1. **Ongoing Mental Health Struggles:** For many people, the effects of bullying don't end when the bullying stops. Anxiety and depression can continue for years after the fact. Victims may have trouble trusting others, forming healthy relationships, or even feeling safe in social situations. In some cases, they might develop PTSD-like symptoms, which can include flashbacks, nightmares, and a constant sense of alertness. This was certainly the case for me.

2. **Trouble with Relationships:** Victims of bullying can struggle with forming and maintaining relationships later in life. The emotional toll bullying takes, like feelings of low self-worth or the fear of being rejected, can make it hard to open up to others. This can lead to more isolation and loneliness, whether in friendships, romantic relationships, or even family connections.

3. **Increased Risk of Substance Abuse:** To cope with the ongoing pain of bullying, some people might turn to unhealthy ways of dealing with their emotions, like drinking or using drugs. Substance abuse can temporarily numb the pain, but it usually ends up making things worse eventually. It can add a whole new layer of physical and emotional damage, making it even harder for the person to heal.

4. **Impact on Careers:** The emotional fallout from bullying will often affect someone's career. The lack of confidence and self-worth that bullying creates can hold someone back from pursuing their goals or reaching their full potential. They may struggle to assert themselves in the workplace, fear failure, or lack motivation, which can affect job performance. In some cases, the long-term effects of bullying can even push someone to change careers or lose their job entirely due to the emotional strain.

Bullying is a severe problem that affects people in both the short and long term. It's not just something that kids go through in school—its impact can last a lifetime. The reasons behind bullying are complex and often involve insecurity, learned behaviours, power struggles, prejudice, and media influence. The effects of bullying can be emotional, social, physical, and academic, with long-term consequences like mental health issues, trouble with relationships, substance abuse, and career challenges.

It's crucial that we all work together to address bullying wherever it happens. Whether it's in schools, workplaces, or online, creating supportive and understanding environments is the first step towards reducing bullying and helping those affected by it. Everyone deserves to feel valued, respected, and safe from harm. By taking action, we can make that happen.

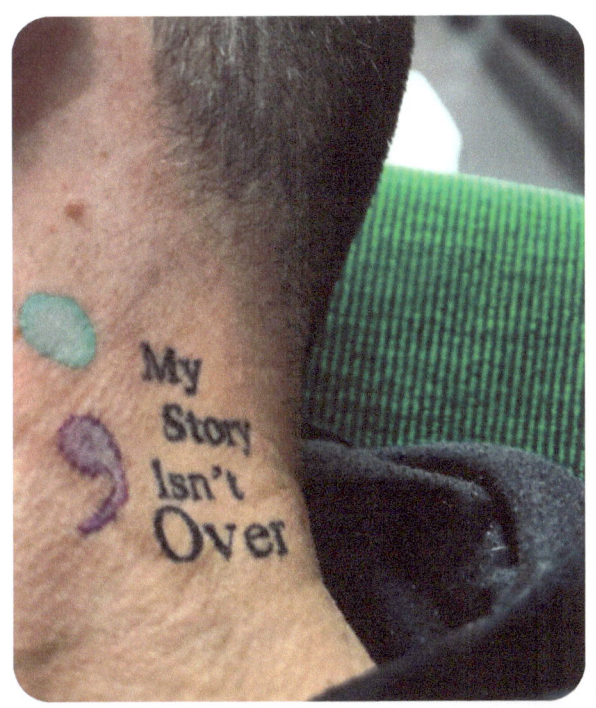

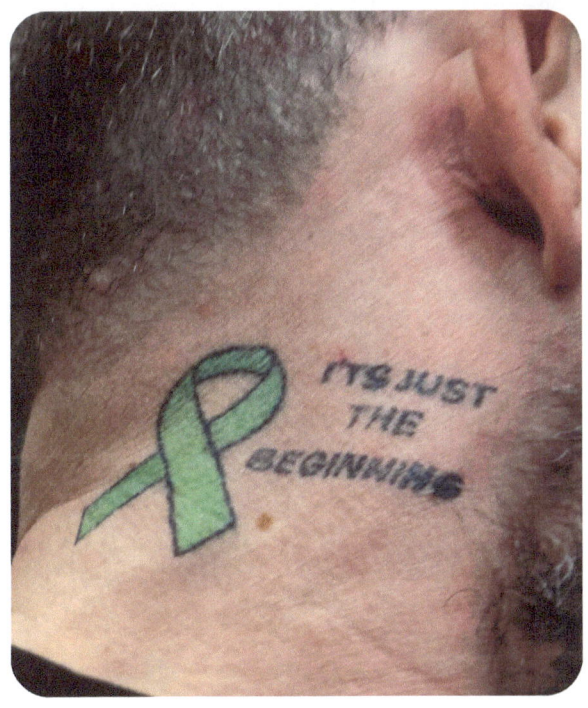

And Finally:

Mine has been a hard journey, and there were times when I felt as though my character was being constantly undermined, with others trying to make me look like a liar. The weight of these false accusations was immense, and it often left me feeling helpless and lost. But through it all, I've come to realise something particularly important – there is one thing, and one thing only, that absolutely nobody can ever take away from me and that is my passion. My drive. The burning desire within me is to not only help myself live a better and more fulfilling life but also to extend my hand to others, no matter where they are in the world. This passion isn't just about personal success or progress – it goes beyond that. It's about sharing my journey with people from all walks of life and showing them that, no matter how difficult the struggles, there is always hope, always a way forward.

Whether it's through my own experiences or by raising funds on my adventures, I've found a purpose that gives me a sense of pride and meaning.

So, while the challenges I've faced may have tried to strip me of certain opportunities, they can never take away the fire within me to make a real difference, to give back, and to continue my mission of improving not just my life, but the lives of others around the globe.

Thank you for reading *The Hardest Walk*. And as for me? Well, my journey isn't over—it's just beginning! My book is dedicated to my grandad. That tall, quiet figure that I first became aware of standing at the gate of my house, talking to my mother, was to be the man who became my hero and helped me understand myself and my life. There really are no words to do justice to a man like my grandad.

I've set up a JustGiving page, where I can help raise money for causes that are close to my heart. Each step I take, every penny I raise, is a reminder that despite all the hardships and setbacks, I'm making a difference. I'm using my voice, my story, and my determination to bring about positive change for others.

www.ingramcontent.com/pod-product-compliance
Lightning Source LLC
Chambersburg PA
CBHW041219070526
44584CB00001B/12